RED ROCK RECOLLECTIONS
VOLUME II

*Fun Historic Stops in
Southern Utah, Northern
Arizona and Southern Nevada*

By Reuben Wadsworth

PUBLISHER'S NOTE:

No part of this book may be reproduced, scanned, or distributed in any printed or electronic form without express written permission from the publisher. The scanning, uploading, and distribution of this book via the Internet or any other means without the permission of the publisher is illegal and punishable by law. Please do not participate in or encourage piracy of copyrighted materials in violation of the author's rights. Purchase only authorized editions.

Text Copyright 2020 ©Reuben Wadsworth
All rights reserved.

Cover Design: Melissa Wadsworth
Map Graphics: Rachael Wilkinson
Editor: Gina Casto
Interior Design: Manon Lavoie
Publisher: Scrivera Press

ISBN: 978-1-7345846-0-8 (Paperback)
First Edition

Hurricane, Utah
Produced in the United States of America
10 9 8 7 6 5 4 3 2 1

Front cover, top: View of the Bryce Canyon amphitheater that greets hikers near the top of the Navajo Loop Trail includes one of the park's most iconic formations, Thor's Hammer, to the left.
Front cover, bottom: The Butch Cassidy Boyhood Home located just south of Circleville, Utah, was restored in 2017 after years of languishing in anonymity and disrepair
Back cover: Lee's Fort next to Lee's Ferry along the Colorado River in Northern Arizona stands as a reminder of the time when the location was an important river crossing.
All cover photos by author

TABLE OF CONTENTS

FORWARD TO VOLUME II

Garret Hobart died in 1899. While his name is unfamiliar to us today, if we lived in late 19th century America, we would easily recognize him.

In 1910, Hobart's biographer would write that Hobart's death "fixed his memory at the height of his fame." Of course, that would prove not to be true.

Hobart served as the Vice President to William McKinley. As Vice President, Hobart proved a capable advisor and a sincere friend to the President and used his role as President of the Senate to effectively and efficiently guide McKinley's legislative agenda through that body.

The death of Hobart devastated McKinley and left a vacancy that would not be filled until the next general election in 1900. The Republican nomination for Vice President in 1900 was almost forced on McKinley by the machinations of the party bosses in New York who were tired of the interference of their progressive governor. That Governor, who would become the Vice President in March 1901 and upon the assassination of William McKinley six months later was Theodore Roosevelt, who would go on to not only significantly change the course of American politics, but the destiny of the nation as well.

Now, I am a public historian. My job is to connect people to the traditions, ideas, and knowledge of the past through oral history, object-based storytelling, and interactive experiences. I often spend time wandering through the Cedar City Cemetery, an amazing piece of local history, however, at times, it can be a frustrating experience. The common practice of placing birth and death dates on headstones is great for the genealogist, but, as a historian, I am interested in the dash in the middle. After all, it is our story that gives meaning to our lives; in a sense, our birth and death are merely mechanical processes. After all, to those of us separated by the years, knowing Garret Hobart's story, that is what truly makes him human to us.

To me, history is a collection of stories. As historians, we search these stories and look for patterns that provide meaning to our experience in an effort to understand who we are, where we came from, and how we can be our best selves. History is built on human experiments. History is made by humans. It acts as a guide, not a predictor. It fashions the human character. Life is only a series of experiences, one occurring after another. It's not the sum total that counts, but how we personally deal with them that ultimately makes the difference as to whether we are happy or not.

Ultimately history is about the story; those things that motivate us, connect us, and bind us together as a wonderfully diverse and expanding society. This collection of essays, stories that explore our local past with new eyes, serves to remind us that the past has power. Memories fade, photographs dim, spoken words are forgotten; however, Reuben's writing reminds us that recording our history, writing our story, is essential to remembering who we are, where we came from, and what we can be. It is my devout belief that humans make history, but an understanding of history makes humans.

Ryan D. Paul
Southern Utah University

ACKNOWLEDGMENTS

In my previous journalism stints, I wrote about sports and the goings-on of several municipalities. While I enjoyed writing about those topics, it wasn't until 2017 that I received the best journalism gig I've ever had.

Knowing my passion for history, Joyce Kuzmanic, former editor-in-chief of *St. George News*, invited me to take over the Days Series, about the histories of interesting places around the Southern Utah, Northern Arizona and Southern Nevada regions. She believed in me and has been one of the biggest fans of the series, giving me plenty of encouragement as the series progressed. For the first year, Joyce was the primary copy editor of these stories.

The articles in this compilation first appeared on the online newspaper *St. George News* and are reprinted with permission from *St. George News* and Canyon Media. I sincerely thank those two entities for granting me that permission so these bits and pieces of Southern Utah history can be enjoyed on the printed page instead of just on a screen.

Also, big thanks go to two other editors at *St. George News* who have been copy editing the stories ever since, Paul Dail and Joseph Witham. They've been catching plenty of typos and minor Associated Press style errors (which isn't my strong suit) and providing me with regular encouragement as well.

Speaking of encouragement, there are four ladies who stand out in that department. Lin Floyd, the Chair of Dixie Poets and with whom I've been collaborating for years on youth poetry contests and creative writing workshops in my capacity as a middle school teacher, told me soon after I took over the series that once I had written enough articles, I should put together a book compilation. She has given me plenty of positive feedback and provided me with numerous pictures that accompanied the articles in their original form.

I met Julie Saemisch, a member of the Zion National Park Forever Project Board who wrote the foreword because of the series and have thoroughly enjoyed getting to know her and have sincerely appreciated her positive feedback and encouragement to get this book published.

Due to my work on the Days Series, I have also had the pleasure to associate with Bobbi Wan-kier, the director of the Silver Reef Museum. Her enthusiasm for local history is extremely keen, even as a transplant from Chicago. Her enthusiasm for my work has been significant.

Another fellow *St. George News* staffer, Hollie Reina, has been a huge fan since Day 1 as well and has helped with pictures and finding the right people to talk to.

Thank you, Lin, Julie, Bobbi and Hollie for your unwavering support!

I am grateful to Ryan Paul, longtime museum director of Frontier Homestead State Park in Cedar City, both for writing the foreword, but also for his help in finding information for most of the stories of places within Iron County, Utah.

I appreciate Rachael Wilkinson's effort in creating the orientation maps that precede each section and for cleaning up my cover to ready it for publication.

My family, of course, has also been a huge support. My mother, Vanda Wadsworth, read many of my stories before they were published and offered great constructive feedback. My father, Carl Wadsworth, has truly been an inspiration for some of these stories and was even a star source for two of them, Smith Mesa and the Hurricane Canal, because he *lived* the history of those two places. Fittingly, the Smith Mesa story, which appears in Volume I, was the first one I wrote for the series and has been one of the stories to garner the most positive feedback.

Both my parents have been huge supports my entire life, and this series was no exception. They have enjoyed hearing me tell them about my latest "adventures" in the series and they even accompanied me on a few of them. I thank my parents for always being there for me.

Some of the biggest thanks go to my wife, Melissa. She has encouraged me and accompanied me on most of these excursions along with our three daughters. It's been a wonderful experience to teach my family the history of our area through our visits to these fascinating places. I appreciate my family's patience with me as our excursions weren't by the book since I was constantly taking pictures and talking to the right people at many of the locations.

Today whenever we visit practically anywhere, one of my daughters inevitably asks, "Dad, are you going to write about this place?" I thank my wife and daughters for always being there for me as well.

I would be remiss if I didn't thank all the kind people who have taken the time to provide me with information and pictures for these stories through in-person, telephone, or email interviews.

I also must thank all of the readers who have joined me vicariously on these journeys. I sincerely appreciate all of the emails, comments and other shows of support that have made the experience of writing this series even more rewarding.

AUTHOR'S NOTE

As the Days Series is written for a general audience and not an academic audience, there are no footnotes or formal citations within the text of these stories. I have cited sources informally by simply stating where I got the information within the text, whether it is a book, article, person, or other source. Where information is in quotations, it is taken word-for-word from the source material. When the author or interviewee is noted (whether he or she "wrote" it or "said" it, etc.), and the information is not in quotations, I am simply summarizing or paraphrasing the author or interviewee and acknowledging that the information came from them.

I did not pour over historical archives or research for hours on end to write these stories. My mantra, however, is to put together a good story from all the readily available sources I can find to provide different points of view. It is vitally important to look at many different sources in historical research to be able to provide the whole picture, and that is what I've tried to do in these pieces even though the "picture" I've created is a brief one.

In essence, the works cited pages for these pieces are within the stories themselves when I list the books and articles from which I got the information. Interviews with experts were also a vital source of information. Additionally, at the end of most stories, I provide some website suggestions for further information.

I took most of the pictures that appear in this compilation and only give photo credit for pictures kindly shared with me by friends or family members.

Additionally, at the beginning of each section are maps to provide readers (especially those unfamiliar with the terrain) with orientation on where each place detailed is located. The numbers in each circle surrounded by a star correspond with the numbers assigned to each chapter.

INTRODUCTION TO VOLUME II

Many of the early European-American settlers of Southern Utah, Northern Arizona, and Southern Nevada came seeking to farm and ranch on what to some of them might have seemed at first an inhospitable wasteland. They struggled to truly "tame" the land. In their struggle to survive, some didn't seem to care much about the surrounding scenery, but little did they know that the breathtaking landscape would be a huge engine of the local economy in the next century.

Today, tourism is vital to the economies of small rural counties in southern Utah. While farming and ranching are still a staple to these local economies, it does not have the same influence as tourism does.

This region still captures the hearts of enthusiasts of American West lore due to its wide expanses of seemingly untamed land but mainly due to its time as the "star" of the show in many movies and television shows of the Western genre, from the silent films of the early 20th century to critically acclaimed works of the genre that have had staying power in the national consciousness such as *Butch Cassidy and the Sundance Kid.*

One of the region's most notable contributions to popular American West history is as the birthplace of the title character of that famous movie—one of the West's most notorious outlaws, born Robert Leroy Parker but better known as Butch Cassidy. He was born in Beaver, Utah, on April 13, 1866, and left his boyhood home in Circleville as a teenager. After that, the well-known bandit didn't actually spend a lot of time in southern Utah during his legendary career.

Tales such as those of "The Robin Hood of the West" is what makes the history of the American West so much fun and such an attraction to the tourists who come to the area hoping to find their own piece of that western story. This volume details plenty of pieces of that history, from the stereotypical, close to what readers have seen in movies and TV shows of the Western genre, such as the story of a rough-and-tumble mining location, Eldorado

Canyon, to the stories behind the filming of some of the most famous of Western films. Some of the stories in this volume are also a bit more atypical, such as the self-contained alleged utopian community of Orderville, who tried but failed to live the law of consecration. The travails of early pioneers are front and center, from a ferry operator whose recommendations to higher-ups often fell on deaf ears to settlers who had to spend the winter living in their wagons.

Two *fun* stories in this volume are about mid-twentieth-century explorations of the region's forbidding geography. Most might assume that by the turn of the 20th century, all of the far reaches of the area had been explored. But the truth is, what would become Goblin Valley and Kodachrome Basin state parks were still blank spots on the map. The respective exploring parties found otherworldly terrain worthy of special protection.

Also, within these annals are stories about the battles to set aside some of these scenic wonderlands as national parks and monuments. There are also tales of competing visions for the fate of these special landscapes, chief among them the fight over the construction of the Glen Canyon Dam, which inundated canyons that will never be seen again.

While many of the locations detailed in this volume are on the map because of their astounding scenery, they have a fascinating history equal to their stunning beauty. The *fun* of American West history is on display at many of them, both authentic, such as the hands-on ranger activities of Pipe Spring National Monument—and inauthentic—such as the Old Bryce Town Shops filled with kitschy, popular Western souvenirs across the highway from Ruby's Inn near the entrance of Bryce Canyon National Park.

Whether authentic or inauthentic, the readers' journey to explore these twenty-six places will certainly be enjoyable, enlightening, and, hopefully, unforgettable.

I.

SOUTHERN UTAH

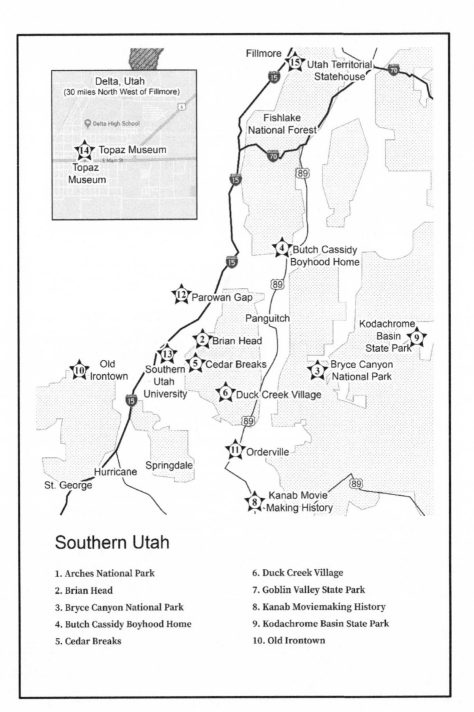

Southern Utah

1. Arches National Park	6. Duck Creek Village
2. Brian Head	7. Goblin Valley State Park
3. Bryce Canyon National Park	8. Kanab Moviemaking History
4. Butch Cassidy Boyhood Home	9. Kodachrome Basin State Park
5. Cedar Breaks	10. Old Irontown

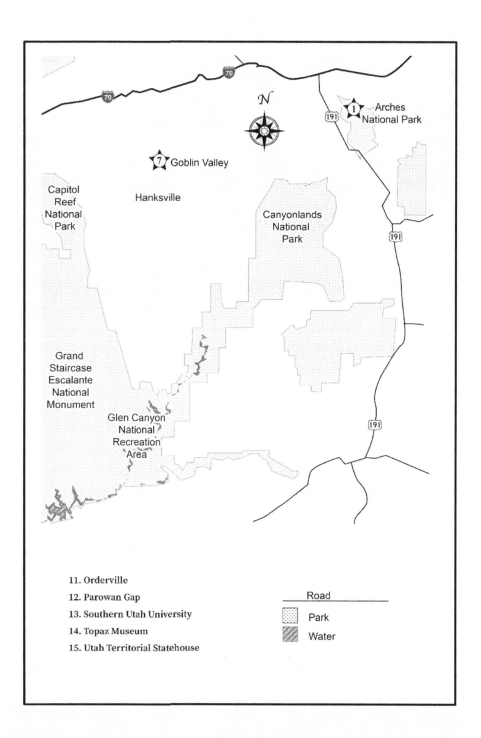

11. Orderville
12. Parowan Gap
13. Southern Utah University
14. Topaz Museum
15. Utah Territorial Statehouse

*Delicate Arch with the snow-capped LaSal Mountains
in the background is one of the most iconic
representations of Arches National Park*

1

ARCHES NATIONAL PARK
A Story of Fanciful Formations, a Polarizing Protector and Troublesome Traffic

The Biscuits, Buccaneer Rock, Dark Angel, Eye-of-the-Whale, Ham Rock, Marching Men, Parade of Elephants, The Three Penguins, Tower of Babel—all these colorful, imaginative names can be found in Arches National Park.

Some are head-scratchers, such as Duck-on-the-Rock, which many visitors might think requires a little too much imagination to agree it actually resembles waterfowl. However, there are other formations that are appropriately named and take practically no imagination to agree their names fit, including Balanced Rock, The Three Gossips, and The Poodle.

To call Arches a grand geologic spectacle is an understatement. Not surprisingly, it contains the largest concentration of natural arches in the world, over 2,000 of them concentrated in just under 77,000 acres, along with many other geologic formations that can take on any number of resemblances, depending on who one asks.

The park website explains how they formed this way:

> *"First, geologic forces wrinkled and folded the buried sandstone, as if it were a giant rug and someone gathered two edges toward each other, making lumps across the middle called Anticlines. As the sandstone warped, fractures tore through it, establishing the patterns for rock sculptures of the future. ...The forces of erosion carved layer after layer of rock away. Once exposed, deeply buried sandstone layers rebounded and expanded, like a sponge expands after its squeezed (though not quite so quickly). This created even more fractures, each one a pathway for water to seep into the rock and further break it down."*

Millions of years of erosion caused by wind and water created this *breakdown* in large fins of Entrada sandstone that carved the arches and other formations visitors see today. Due to constant erosive forces, all arches will eventually fall, just as Wall Arch in Devil's Garden did in 2008.

Other more recent major events showcasing the constant erosion in the park was when Skyline Arch doubled in size after a large boulder fell from it in 1940. Additionally, a sixty-foot slab fell from Landscape Arch in 1991.

Native Americans

Native Americans did not live in what is now Arches National Park, but there is plenty of evidence of their forays into it. They used the land to quarry chert for making arrow points and other chipped stone implements. They also searched for food in what is now the park. What they thought of its scenery will always be speculation, John Hoffman noted in his book *Arches National Park: An Illustrated Guide.*

Fun Historic Stops in Southern Utah

The Archaic Indians, whose culture lasted from about 8,000 to 3,000 years ago, were hunter-gatherers who lived in small, kin-related bands. Evidence of the Archaic is in split-twig figurines fashioned to resemble animals, which were found ten miles southeast of the park in Moonshine Cave on the north bank of Mill Creek.

Anthropologists have suggested that they were used as fetishes "to invoke magical powers for successful hunts," Hoffman wrote.

Starting at around 1000 A.D., the Fremont and Anasazi people populated the area. Different than the Archaic, they engaged in agriculture and left petroglyphs and cliff dwellings in the area similar to those found in Mesa Verde National Park. The Utes were the Native Americans that the first settlers from The Church of Jesus Christ of Latter-day Saints encountered when they arrived in the area in the mid-19th century.

Early Settlers

No one knows the true identity of the first white man to set eyes on what is now Arches National Park, but there are plenty of possibilities. The first possible penetration by Europeans could have been a party led by Juan Maria Antonio Rivera, who traipsed through the territory in 1765 in search of silver. Another Spanish expedition that came in 1813 to trade with the Utes along the Sevier River could have entered what is now Arches, Hoffman wrote. Those traveling the Old Spanish Trail in the 1830s and 1840s probably came close to the park and forded the river near its present-day boundary.

In 1855, the Huntington Expedition, led by William Huntington, whose purpose was to explore the area and speak with the Navajos, came through Moab Canyon on the park's western border. This group came to a "jump" where the wagons had to be let down by ropes to traverse the precarious drop. That "jump" was located just across the highway from where the visitor center stands but was eliminated through grading during the construction of U.S. Highway 191.

The first attempt at settlement came just after the Huntington Expedition and became known as the Elk Mountain Mission, named for the nearby mountain range now known as the La Sal

Mountains. This group built a rock fort and a log corral near a grove of cottonwood trees at the northwest corner of the current town of Moab, but their attempt was short-lived as Indian hostilities broke out, killing three of the potential settlers causing them to pack up and leave. Permanent settlement did not take place for another twenty years, the result of efforts by ranchers, prospectors, and farmers.

In 1880, Henry Penney started operating a small ferry to cross the Colorado River near the location of today's Moab Bridge. A few years later, Norman Taylor began another ferryboat operation, but in 1897, Grand County took over the service with a larger ferryboat, which operated until 1912 when the first bridge to span the river was completed.

Possibly the first settlers within what is now Arches National Park were John Wolfe and his son, Fred, who established a ranch in 1898 where the Delicate Arch Trailhead is now. The elder Wolfe was a Civil War veteran who injured his leg at the Battle of Vicksburg in 1863, requiring the use of a crutch for the rest of his life. The pair came from Ohio. It is unknown what inspired them to establish a ranch in the desolate location or how they even knew about it, Hoffman wrote. One theory is that they came seeking a drier climate, which might have improved the pain in the senior Wolfe's leg.

A small seventeen-foot by fifteen-foot cabin they built in 1906, fashioned from cottonwood logs, still stands today (a flash flood destroyed an earlier cabin). They also built a corral, a dam for irrigation water, and a root cellar, used for storage of root crops and other vegetables.

The pair left in 1910 and several other ranchers used the cabin until it was acquired by the National Park Service in 1948.

National Park Status

There are several men who can take some credit for literally putting Arches on the map, leading to its designation as a national monument first, then a national park. John "Doc" Williams, Moab's local doctor in the late 19th and early 20th century did a lot to promote the conservation of natural wonders in South-eastern Utah. Another early advocate of the Arches landscape was Loren "Bish" Taylor, who, as Moab's newspaper editor, regularly let his readers know about the beauty of the surrounding scenery. Taylor loved exploring and describing the rock wonderland just north of the frontier town.

Hungarian immigrant Alexander Ringhoffer also became a significant advocate of Arches and became, in Hoffman's mind, "the Father of Arches." The miner and prospector made his first expedition into what is now Arches with his sons and son-in-law in December 1922, visiting what is now known as Klondike Bluffs, which he called "Devil's Garden."

After seeing the vast array of spectacular sandstone monuments, Ringhoffer contacted representatives of the Denver and Rio Grande Railroad, encouraging their representatives to see the area. Ringhoffer personally escorted railroad representatives on jaunts into what is now the park to show them its natural wonders and to photograph them. Frank Wadleigh, the Denver and Rio Grande's passenger traffic manager, personally wrote to the first National Park Service Director, Stephen Mather, extolling the virtues of the land and suggesting it become a national monument, according to Hoffman.

A government surveyor ventured into the area but mistakenly thought what is now known as "The Windows" (what Ringhoffer called "Window Castles") and Ringhoffer's "Devil's Garden" were the same place. Moab's newspaper presented an article detailing that survey and photos from it, which Wadleigh saw, causing him to write to Mather about the geographical discrepancy.

Coincidentally, a later government surveyor examined the fins and arches on the east ridge of Salt Valley, which he thought was Ringhoffer's "Devil's Garden," so he gave it that name. This is the name that stuck for this locale, and the Devil's Garden of Ringhoffer's imagination became Klondike Bluffs instead.

All name confusion aside, it was Ringhoffer's efforts that brought Arches into the consciousness of the right people to preserve it. Mather made a formal recommendation for Arches to become a national monument in January 1926, but the Secretary of the

Interior at the time, Hubert Work, opposed adding more national monuments, advocating the return of some national monuments to the states to become state parks instead, Hoffman wrote.

Ray Lyman Wilbur, the Secretary of the Interior, appointed by Herbert Hoover, who was elected in 1928, was much more favorable to Mather's plans for Arches. Only a month after the administration took office, Wilbur recommended that Hoover sign an executive order creating Arches National Monument. That signature occurred on April 12, 1929, setting aside 4,250 acres in two detached sections, The Windows, containing 1,920 acres, and Devil's Garden, with 2,600 acres, Hoffman reported. The man responsible for the monument's name was Frank Pinkley, who was the monument's first superintendent. He originally suggested the name in a 1925 letter to Mather.

Interestingly, when Arches first gained national monument status, it did not include the very area that started the push to protect it, Ringhoffer's "Devil's Garden." President Franklin D. Roosevelt expanded the monument to 33,680 acres in 1938, which encompassed what is now Klondike Bluffs.

Many of the park's most enduring names came as a result of a scientific expedition in the park in the winter of 1933-1934 led by Frank Beckwith, editor of the *Millard County Chronicle*. Beckwith named some of its most prominent features, including Delicate Arch, Landscape Arch, and Tower Arch.

Delicate Arch is one of the most famous natural arches in the world and a Utah icon, appearing on its license plates and its National Park quarter. John Van Cott, in his book, *Utah Place Names*, called it "one of the grandest and most photogenic of Utah's natural arches." Early cowboys called the arch "The Schoolmarm's Pants," or "Bloomer's Arch" and other names, but the present name demonstrates "a more artistic, aesthetic approach," Van Cott wrote.

But Delicate Arch might have been a more accurate name for the park's Landscape Arch or Skyline Arch. As noted previously, large slabs of rock have fallen from both their spans in the last eighty years. Another arch that is delicate in the park is Broken Arch, which has a narrow crack in its crest.

Fun Historic Stops in Southern Utah

In Arches' early years, transportation was a challenge as there were no paved roads. Early superintendents complained of the bad roads that included a lot of ruts that couldn't be graded until they were wet, right after a rainstorm.

Ringhoffer himself was the first to access Arches via an automobile on his excursions with railroad officials. Harry Goulding was the first to drive into Arches after its designation as a national monument, outfitting his Ford with special tires to better negotiate the sand.

In the 1940s and 1950s, traversing Courthouse Wash could be treacherous. Several times during that span, it flooded, stranding numerous motorists. Starting in 1958, road projects began that eventually resulted in 26.5 miles of paved roads, "providing motorists entry into rugged terrain which previously had been largely inaccessible," including The Windows and Devil's Garden, Hoffman wrote.

"Managers of the park knew in the 1940s that Arches would become more and more of an attraction because it was right off of a major highway (now U.S. 191)," said Arches' Archivist and Collections Manager Peekay Briggs.

Improved transportation led to expanding visitation as well as even greater protection as the park was doubled in 1969 by President Lyndon B. Johnson's administration. It achieved national park status just over two years later, on November 16, 1971, during the Richard Nixon Administration.

Arches' Most Famous Advocate

During the 1956 and 1957 seasons, Arches National Monument's lone seasonal ranger living in a little trailer near Balanced Rock would start his trajectory of becoming one of the most controversial environmentalists in U.S. history. Arches was his main inspiration.

In fact, author Terry Tempest Williams called Edward Abbey the "Mark Twain of the American desert," stating that he had "bad behavior and big-hearted ideas."

In his article in a winter 2018 issue of *National Parks* magazine, marking the 50th anniversary of Abbey's most revered work,

Hikers gather under North Window, who,
with its nearby 'twin,' is the namesake of
"The Windows" section of Arches National Park

Desert Solitaire (first published in 1968), Todd Christopher wrote that Abbey had an "anarchistic brand of environmental advocacy that makes him a polarizing figure to this day—and one can't help but feel that's the way he'd like it."

"It's not just a love letter to the land," Christopher explained of *Desert Solitaire*. "Abbey's physically and psychologically vivid portrait of the desert became a rallying cry for its preservation against the forces of development."

Edward Abbey was to Arches what John Muir was to Yosemite, a fierce protector and advocate. To them, the two respective parks they loved were sacred: nature's cathedrals.

One of the main messages Abbey tried to get across in *Desert Solitaire* is that national parks need to be protected and left the way nature intended them, without large-scale development. If Abbey would have had his way, for instance, there would be no cars in national parks.

"The motorized tourists, reluctant to give up the old ways, will complain that they can't see enough without their automobiles to bear them swiftly (traffic permitting) through the parks," Abbey wrote. "But this is nonsense. A man on foot, on horseback or on a bicycle will see more, feel more, enjoy more in one mile than the motorized tourists can in one hundred miles."

In a sense, Abbey considered his writing in *Desert Solitaire* an obituary.

"Most of what I write about in this book is already gone or going under fast," he wrote in the book's preface. "This is not a travel guide but an elegy. A memorial."

Many would consider Abbey extremely prescient in his foresight.

In perhaps the most famous chapter of the book, entitled "Polemic: Industrial Tourism and the National Parks," Christopher wrote that "Abbey prophesies and decries a future where the parks are overrun by motorized tourists and reduced to little more than theme parks."

One of the places near Arches where Abbey's legacy is alive and well is at Back of Beyond Books, a bookstore that derives its name from a phrase used in Abbey's novel, "The Monkey Wrench Gang," and which features an entire bookcase devoted to his works prominently located just inside the front door.

According to Christopher's story, the bookstore is a place where Abbey "continues to find an audience" because it sells six hundred to seven hundred copies of *Desert Solitaire* a year.

In contrast to those who pay homage to him in Moab, just over five miles up the road at Arches National Park headquarters, Abbey has almost no presence in the park's archives or historical record, Briggs noted.

"There was some interest where his trailer was located, but most other mentions in our records are random newspaper clippings," Briggs explained. "In the words of the former museum curator, 'Arches was far more important to Abbey than Abbey was to Arches.' And as far as I can tell, no one has been able to disprove that statement, although some fans like to claim anecdotal evidence because Abbey is important to them."

It would be easy to guess that Abbey would be flabbergasted by what he would see in Arches today with the traffic congestion caused by crushing visitation.

Erosive forces will eventually carve these sandstone fins near Sand Dune Arch into future arches

Modern Challenges

Challenges Arches has experienced over the last twenty to thirty years are the same challenges that other iconic parks face, including Zion, Grand Canyon, and Yosemite, Briggs said.

"We must balance between protecting cultural and natural resources and allowing for visitor enjoyment and access—Arches is not unique in that respect," Briggs said.

Case in point is the line of cars waiting to enter the park on busy weekends, which, in some cases, has necessitated closing the park for a few hours at a time. That is not the kind of experience park visitors are expecting and is a definite drag on visitor enjoyment. To rectify this situation, Arches is looking at options similar to what Zion is currently considering—an advanced reservation system and even a mandatory shuttle system similar to Zion's. Paving the Salt Valley or Willow Springs roads at the north end of the park to create another entrance has also been discussed.

The increase in visitation is detrimental to the traffic and parking situation and a problem away from the pavement as well. Due to the overuse of the Fiery Furnace, the park implemented a reservation system, which resulted in some controversy, Briggs noted. It has also implemented a reservation system in its lone campground near Devil's Garden.

The park has also experienced an increase in social trails—trails caused by hikers not sticking on designated paths—and has ramped up education efforts to inform visitors not to step on biological crust, formerly known as "cryptobiotic soil," Briggs explained. This important soil layer consists of living organisms such as lichens, moss, and bacteria that literally keeps the soil together and helps reduce erosion.

As with many other national parks, it is easy for park management to diagnose Arches' problems. It's the remedy for them that is difficult, largely due to lack of funding.

"We compete for funding at almost every level—against other agencies and within the NPS and even within the park—what divisions get the share of that funding and how we are allowed to use some of it," Briggs said. "In order to preserve the characteristics of the park, and to follow legislation mandating protections, we have to know and understand the resources. In the past thirty years, Arches, as part of the Southeast Utah Group, has built a Resource Stewardship and Science division to study and protect park resources."

In fact, one of the things that could steer the park away from a mandatory shuttle is funding, especially for maintenance of the fleet.

One can guarantee, though, that one solution to Arches' crushing visitation that Abbey might have advocated will never come to pass: eliminating cars altogether. Such a solution would be completely against one of the founding mandates of the NPS to provide access and enjoyment to the parks for all Americans.

Double Arch (center right) stands among other rock formations in the Windows Section of Arches National Park

Visiting Arches

Arches is an approximate four-hour, forty-five-minute drive from the St. George area by heading north on Interstate 15 until its intersection with Interstate 70, then following I-70 east until Exit 182, where southbound U.S. 191 leads to the park entrance just over twenty-six miles from the exit.

Arches boasts a variety of hikes, many of which are ideal for families with young children. For instance, kids will enjoy strolling down Park Avenue and exploring The Windows as well as playing in the sand at Sand Dune Arch.

Two of the most popular trails are Devil's Garden (which includes Landscape Arch) and Delicate Arch. Fiery Furnace is also popular, but, as previously mentioned, visitors need an advance reservation to hike through it.

Those desiring to hike popular trails will want to arrive early to ensure a parking spot or delay their hike until later in the afternoon. As a general rule, parking is most congested from 10 a.m. to 2 p.m.

The best times to visit are fall, spring, and winter as summer temperatures can be scorching. During the winter, visitors will see the smallest crowds and have the opportunity to see the formations with a different perspective, a light dusting of snow.

Fun Historic Stops in Southern Utah

The original story and photo gallery can be found at the following link:

https://www.stgeorgeutah.com/news/archive/2019/11/17/raw-arches-history-day-a-story-of-fanciful-formations-a-polarizing-protector-and-troublesome-traffic/

FOR FURTHER INFORMATION

Arches National Park website

https://www.nps.gov/arch/index.htm

*Georg's Ski Shop is still operated today
by Brian Head's founding family*

2

BRIAN HEAD
The Families at the Heart of Utah's Highest Ski Resort

It might surprise some Southern Utah residents to know that Brian Head—at ninety-eight hundred feet—boasts the highest base elevation of any ski resort in Utah even though it is the southernmost. Brian Head town, not surprisingly, is the highest incorporated municipality in the state.

Both high-altitude entities have worked in concert for over forty years and could not exist without the other.

No one knows for sure just exactly how Brian Head Peak, first known as Bear Flats and Monument Peak, got its name. One theory is that the name derived from the three-time Democratic presidential candidate of the late 1800s and early 1900s, William Jennings Bryan. Another is that the name came from a Parowan family with the surname of Bryan, while another says a man named Bryan built a monument up on the rock (head) of the mountain. Brian Head Resort's "our history" webpage cites yet another story that claims explorer John Wesley Powell saw the peak above all the others and named it after an official in the Geographical Survey Office by the name of Bryan—an idea supported by author Rufus Wood Leigh in his 1860s book, *Five Hundred Utah Place Names*.

However Brian Head first got its name, one thing is for sure: The Y in Bryan was dropped in favor of an I.

In the late 19th and early 20th centuries, the area was known as "Little Ireland" for the Adams family of Irish heritage, who used the area for dairying and as a summer grazing range for sheep and horses. It was also the site of some logging. In the 1920s, it boasted a hotel, restaurant, and dance hall operated by Minnie Adams Burton, known as Minnie's Mansion. The spot was popular for its huge breakfasts, fireworks, and dancing.

In the 1930s, brothers Thomas and Joseph Holyoak, from Parowan, acquired the property.

Early Resort History

Real estate developer Burt Nichols got the idea of a ski resort in Southern Utah off to a start in the early 1960s. He considered other spots on Cedar Mountain, including the Navajo Lake area, as well as some out-of-state places such as Williams and Flagstaff, Arizona, and Mt. Charleston, Nevada, but settled on Brian Head mainly because roads already reached it, it was close to Interstate 15, and at the time, Bonanza Airlines and the Union Pacific Railroad serviced Cedar City.

Cedar City resident Milt Jolley helped convince the reluctant Holyoak brothers to sell their land after taking them to a ski resort in California and showing them how a ski resort would benefit the Parowan economy.

Nichols teamed up with a group of investors and formed the Brian Head Corporation in May 1964 and, with a loan from the Small Business Administration, constructed the first facilities, a seven-hundred-vertical-foot chairlift, a three-hundred-vertical-foot T-bar lift and a warming house starting in September 1964.

The first two permanent buildings were a clinic owned by Dr. David Wilkerson of Cedar City and Georg and Stefanie Hartlmaier's home and rental shop. The first season, two mobile homes were leased to be a warming house, restrooms, and an eating area.

The resort opened in January 1965. As part of its outreach to generate interest among the local population, the resort set up a four-week ski training program to familiarize Iron County youth with skiing. It invited youths ages ten to eighteen to participate in lessons every Saturday morning for only $6 for the whole month. A season pass during that first season was only $21 for an adult and $13 for youths fifteen and under.

Despite favorable snow conditions, positive press, and a massive advertising campaign in nearby population centers such as Los Angeles, Las Vegas, and Phoenix, Brian Head struggled to attract skiers during its first season, and those it did attract were mostly locals. Thankfully, word-of-mouth advertising after the first season attracted many more skiers the second season and revenue increased by nearly seventy-five percent that second year.

During the resort's early history, the small staff was required to go above and beyond, taking on many different duties. One of those early staff members who made a major contribution in Brian Head's early days was Mel Hunter, who was not even a skier. A retired foreman of the U.S. Steel mines, Hunter was mainly responsible for keeping the slopes well-packed with his snow-mobile, often packing snow until late in the night and waking up at 3-4 a.m. the next day to make ready for skiers. Hunter also fixed broken machinery, ran chairlifts, oversaw the rental shop, and whatever else he was asked to do.

The resort did not significantly expand until the 1969-1970 season when a new 1,190-vertical-foot lift was installed running east up the mountain that could handle nine hundred skiers every hour.

Herman "Chip" Deutschlander, whose family operates Brian Head Sports, said Brian Head has come a long way in forty years because when he and his family arrived at the resort in 1976, there were not even parking lots—people just parked at the side of the road—and the chairlifts had wooden seats.

*A ski bridge and lift frames Georg's Ski Shop
at Brian Head Resort*

"Mr. Brian Head" and His Family

Nichols knew he needed an experienced skier to direct the future resort's ski operations and went looking for a good-looking European man who could speak English to help him do just that. Fate took him to the sporting goods store, Sport Scheck, in Munich, where he found the man who fit the bill to a tee: Georg Hartlmaier. Nichols invited Hartlmaier to dinner and showed him pictures of the Brian Head area. Despite offers from two other American resorts, Hartlmaier chose Brian Head.

Hartlmaier originally came to Brian Head in 1964 as the resort's first mountain manager and ski school director. He planned the runs, selected the equipment, and helped build the resort's first ski lift.

He and his wife, Stefanie, learned English when they lived in Marin County, California, from 1958 to 1962. The two of them met while attending dances in their hometowns of Hausham and Schliersee, Germany, which are only 1 kilometer apart. When the couple returned to Germany from California, they married on April 23, 1963.

They raised their three children at Brian Head—Georg Jr., Robby, and Stefanie Jr. Stefanie Hartlmaier Sr. said that when they arrived at Brian Head, there was nothing there. At first, the young family lived in Cedar City while their shop and house above it were built at Brian Head. At that time, she wondered if they had made the right decision. But after they moved into their home at the resort in December 1965, she felt right at home and has never left. The Hartlmaiers were the first permanent resident family of Brian Head nearly ten years before it was incorporated as a town.

"We were the pioneers up here for sure," Stefanie Hartlmaier Sr. said.

Both Stefanie Hartlmaier Sr. and Georg Hartlmaier Jr. remember fondly the day Robby Hartlmaier was born, February 18, 1966. A lift operator announced over the resort's public-address system that the population of Brian Head had just increased from three to four.

Utilities were a challenge in those early days. To get water, Stefanie Hartlmaier Sr. said they connected a hose to a nearby spring, and their electricity came from a gas-powered generator. When power came in late 1966, it was a big deal, and it opened the door for the resort and town's future development.

Georg Hartlmaier Sr. literally became the face of Brian Head. His kindness, gregariousness, and looks won over resort-goers. His wife said he even earned the nickname "Mr. Brian Head" as well as "The Stein Eriksen of Brian Head" in a nod to the skiing legend. Fittingly, a picture of Georg Hartlmaier Sr. skiing appeared on the resort's first publicity poster. Later, he was even featured in Warren Miller ski films.

The ski shop, located at the bottom of the resort's first lift, was small at first. They sold ski gear as well as sweaters that Stefanie Hartlmaier Sr. knitted herself. Georg Hartlmaier Sr. entertained Brian Head guests at the shop singing while accompanying himself on the guitar.

For the first eight years, Stefanie Hartlmaier Sr. was in charge of the shop while her husband served as the resort's ski school director, then he concentrated his time on the shop. She said it was nice to be close to the kids while running the shop, always knowing they were only one floor above.

"It was really pretty quiet in the early days," said Georg Hartlmaier Jr., who was two when he put on his first set of skis; those skis are now on display at the shop. "Dad kept us pretty busy."

Georg Hartlmaier Jr. said he was ecstatic when Bill Thompson became general manager of the resort and brought his family, two children, Chris and Heidi, which included giving him a few playmates. He remembers fondly riding the bus, an old yellow converted hearse, down the canyon to go to school in Parowan.

When not skiing and running the shop, Georg Hartlmaier Sr. was outdoors as much as he could be. His first love was not skiing; it was actually mountain climbing, his wife said. He climbed Mount Everest in 1988 but never made it to the summit. He did climb to the top of two other Himalayan Peaks, however: Mount Manaslu and Mount Makalu.

Georg Hartlmaier Sr. loved Zion and Bryce Canyon national parks. Whenever he had company from Germany, he would always take them to those two places.

In 1991, Georg Hartlmaier Sr. suffered a stroke but recovered well and returned to his normal activities for another decade. In 2001 came the diagnosis of Alzheimer's Disease. While it meant the end of his involvement in the shop's day-to-day operations, it could not keep him off the slopes. Georg Hartlmaier Sr. skied until 2006 and died July 6, 2008.

Stefanie Hartlmaier Sr. had always hoped that her sons would return to run the shop. She got her wish as both sons and their wives eventually moved back home to manage the shop after being away for a while to try other things. She said that by luck they both returned and are now totally in charge of the shop. A spunky and witty lady in her eighties, Stefanie Hartlmaier Sr. continued to do the shop's payroll until 2017.

As the family looks back over their many years at Brian Head, they say they have forged incredible friendships with "beautiful people."

From the beginning, Stefanie Hartlmaier Sr. said, Cedar City and Parowan residents have totally embraced the Hartlmaiers despite them not being members of The Church of Jesus Christ of Latter-day Saints, the dominant religion in the region. She explained how fourteen Parowan families invited her to stay with them when Robby was born—an example of the community's tremendous hospitality.

"I never had a day I felt bad that I came," she said. "We made a good decision."

Today the shop is not only a ski and snowboard shop. Starting in the early 1980s, it got into the mountain biking business—even before the resort began allowing mountain bikers to ride its lifts.

Georg Hartlmaier Jr. said when they first started to accommodate mountain bikers, they outfitted the bed of a truck with benches to take them and their bikes up the mountain so they could enjoy the ride down. The resort itself started running lifts for summer mountain biking in the early 1990s. During that same time period, the resort added snowmaking, which has been a boon to the resort and helps it make it through seasons when not enough natural snow falls.

The shop also rents a few cabins for skier accommodations.

"We've done everything except snowmobiles," Georg Hartlmaier Jr. said. "That's the only thing we haven't dabbled in."

Brian Head Today

The Deutschlanders are the Hartlmaiers' competitors across the highway near the base of the Giant Steps lift, but one would not know it by observing their relationship. The two families are the best of friends and regularly have Sunday dinner together, Georg Hartlmaier Jr. said, adding that there is "a little bit of egging every once in a while" over business.

Chip Deutschlander said that if he does not have something for a customer, he calls the Hartlmaiers (and the Hartlmaiers do likewise) to see if they have it because both families have the same goal in mind.

"We want to make sure everyone has a great time," Chip Deutschlander said.

The Deutschlanders have been fixtures in Brian Head since the mid-1970s, and their patriarch, Herman "Dutch" Deutschlander,

The Giant Steps quad lift, pictured here in January 2018,
is also home to a snow tubing hill

was also a mainstay in the government of the town (which incorporated in 1975) as a town council member and mayor. He was recently honored for his forty years of service to the town and was instrumental in helping to bring the sewer and water lines that allowed the town to continue to grow, his son said.

That growth started in the 1980s when large hotel and condominium complexes were built, and the popularity of the resort has now grown in its major markets of southern Nevada and southern California.

Both the Hartlmaiers and Deutschlanders said they have liked where Brian Head's previous owner, John Grissinger, has taken the resort, bringing in new customers and initiating new programs based on visitor feedback as well as replacing the old Giant Steps lift with a high-speed quad.

In November 2019, Grissinger sold the resort to Colorado-based Mountain Capital Partners, which owns several other resorts in Colorado and New Mexico as well as Nordic Valley Ski Resort in Northern Utah.

Visiting Brian Head

Brian Head is approximately an hour-and-a-half drive north of St. George, traveling I-15 northbound to the first Parowan exit (Exit 75), then taking State Route 143 up Parowan Canyon to the resort. For those traveling from the north on I-15, it will be the second Parowan exit, also Exit 75.

In the winter, the resort features eight chairlifts for skiing and snowboarding and also offers tubing.

In the summer, Brian Head Resort is now a mecca for mountain biking as well as numerous other activities, from scenic lift rides to disc golf.

The original story and photo gallery can be found at the following link:

https://www.stgeorgeutah.com/news/archive/2018/02/11/brian-head-day-these-families-are-at-the-heart-of-utahs-highest-ski-resort/

FOR FURTHER INFORMATION
Brian Head Resort website

https://www.brianhead.com/

*Bryce Point offers visitors one of the most sweeping views
of the collection of hoodoos and other formations contained in
Bryce Canyon National Park's main amphitheater*

3

BRYCE CANYON
A Grand Erosive Spectacle With an Identity Crisis

It's a natural amphitheater, not a canyon.

Utah's second national park, a stunning showcase of erosive forces that formed colorful rock pinnacles and spires known as hoodoos, has always had somewhat of an identity crisis.

In the early 20th century, some referred to it as "Temple of the Gods," but that was too close to "Garden of the Gods," just west of Colorado Springs. Others called it "Bryce's Canyon" as if its namesake—who only made his home in the area for approximately five years—owned it.

Back in 1920, the Utah State Automobile Association staged a contest to rename it, concluding that its name was too common for a place so grand.

Garfield County, however, put up a fuss, saying it should have the most say in the naming of its best attraction. The contest went on undaunted, however, but in the end, its judges felt that the names submitted by its entrants weren't up to par and scrapped the rebranding idea in favor of keeping it Bryce Canyon.

Even though the park's name is a misnomer, visitors don't seem to mind as they stroll along the rim of its main amphitheater and traipse down its trails that reach the amphitheater floor.

Early Human Contact

Paiutes and their ancestors have roamed the area for centuries, and settlers of The Church of Jesus Christ of Latter-day Saints were the first Euro-Americans to see the amphitheater's grandeur in the 19th century.

In the early 1870s, members of the Wheeler Survey, a government corps sent to explore and map the Western U.S. west of the 100th meridian became the second set of European Americans to gaze atop what one member of the survey, Grove Karl Gilbert, called "The Summit of the Rim," as he described it in his diary.

"Just before starting down the slope, we caught a glimpse of a perfect wilderness of red pinnacles, the most stunning thing out of a picture," Gilbert wrote, as quoted in a Historical Resource Study about Bryce Canyon by Nicholas Scrattish published in 1985.

One of the most poetic early descriptions of the canyon that's actually an amphitheater came on November 18, 1876, from U. S. Deputy Surveyor T. C. Bailey.

"There are thousands of red, white, purple, and vermilion colored rocks, of all sizes, resembling sentinels on the walls of castles, monks and priests in their robes, attendants, cathedrals, and congregations," Bailey wrote. "There are deep caverns and rooms resembling ruins of prisons, castles, churches with their guarded walls, battlements, spires, and steeples, niches and recesses, presenting the wildest and most wonderful scene that the eye of man ever beheld, in fact, it is one of the wonders of the world."

Despite these superlatives from early explorers, neither early LDS reconnaissance nor the 1870s Federal surveys directed much public attention to the Bryce Canyon region during this time period, Scrattish wrote.

"The Mormons did begin settlement near the eastern edge of the park in 1874, but this did nothing to directly popularize Bryce Canyon's uniqueness," Scrattish wrote. "To some extent, Bryce Canyon's obscurity, until the second decade of the 20th century, can be attributed to its distance from railways and sizeable towns."

In 1875 or 1876, the park's namesake, Ebenezer Bryce, settled in what was known as Clifton (Cliff town) because of its close proximity to the nearby pink cliffs. He became disenchanted with the settlement and moved upstream along Paria Creek to Henderson Valley, building a seven-mile long irrigation ditch to make farming possible.

"Bryce was also instrumental in building a road to make nearby timber and firewood more accessible," Scrattish wrote. "Local people began to use the road and customarily called the amphitheater, at which the road terminated, 'Bryce's Canyon.'"

Bryce's motive for moving to the area was due to his wife's fragile health, but he realized the climate was not as suitable as once thought and moved to Arizona in 1880, at the time not realizing the legacy he would leave on the amphitheater he called "a helluva a place to lose a cow."

By most accounts, the area's first settlers were not that impressed with the one-of-a-kind landscape that enveloped them, which completely astounded 20th century chroniclers of Bryce Canyon, Scrattish noted.

"In fairness to these people, it is, perhaps, more just to empathize with the spirit of a different time—to perceive the situation as they perceived it," Scrattish surmised. "Mormon pioneers in the Bryce Canyon region were an assiduous, God-fearing group, whose struggle against the harsh realities of everyday life left little psychic energy for an appreciation of magnificent scenery."

In the early 20th century, especially the late teens, Bryce Canyon started garnering attention, significantly aided by its proximity to Zion and the Grand Canyon's North Rim, which formed a scenic tourist "loop." Another factor in its popularization was "an uneven but tangible improvement in the area's roads," Scrattish noted.

"A sprinkling of Mormon settlements east and northwest of Bryce Canyon brought with them inadvertent explorers of lesser-known byways, such as salesmen, [who] were destined to drive some of the first automobiles into Tropic and Cannonville," Scrattish wrote. "Their accounts of the area encouraged visits by others."

The Forest Service also played a role in publicizing Bryce's fanciful landscape.

Forest Service Supervisor J.H. Humphrey enlisted Mark Anderson, foreman of the Forest Service grazing crew, to publicize it. When Anderson saw it for the first time, accounts note that he immediately rode into Panguitch and telegrammed the District Forester in Ogden requesting that Forest Service photographer George Coshen be sent to Bryce Canyon with still and movie cameras to capture the grazing crew working near the amphitheater's rim. Coshen sent his movie and still pictures to Forest Service officials in the District of Columbia. The pictures were also made available to Union Pacific Railroad officials in Omaha.

Arthur Stevens, another member of the Forest Service grazing crew, wrote a short, illustrated article for *Outdoor Life*, an early Union Pacific publication, in late 1916. Humphrey also dictated an article for *Red Book*, a Denver and Rio Grande Western Railroad periodical, publishing it under a pseudonym. These stories were the first descriptive articles published about Bryce Canyon.

In 1917, C.B. Hawley, director of the Utah State Automobile Association, visited Bryce Canyon and reported about it to the association's officers in Salt Lake City. Another director of the organization visited soon after to confirm Hawley's report and returned with an even more glowing report. These two directors and State Senator William Seegmiller of Kanab encouraged *Salt Lake Tribune* photographer Oliver Grimes to visit and take pictures.

Grimes's full-page article, titled "Utah's New Wonderland," appeared in the Sunday Magazine section of the "Tribune" on August 25, 1918, and was probably read by more people than anything previously written on Bryce Canyon, Scrattish wrote.

The article said the soon-to-be park was now open to automobile traffic and gave explicit directions to it from Panguitch.

The Original Ruby

In the spring of 1916, when the Forest Service started publicizing Bryce Canyon, Reuben (Ruby) Syrett and his wife, Clara (Minnie), lived in Panguitch but had been scouting the area to start a ranch. The couple decided to homestead a quarter section near Bryce Canyon, approximately 3.5 miles north of what is now Sunset Point. The story goes that the Syretts were there six weeks before a Tropic rancher introduced them to the amphitheater's rim.

The sight left them speechless.

Soon the couple started to invite their friends in Panguitch, who thought they were foolish to homestead in such an area, to see the amphitheater. Despite this, the Syretts hung on to their homestead claim and even started to purchase additional land near it.

In 1919 as word started to spread that Bryce Canyon's beauty was worth a visit, a large group from Salt Lake City came and were accommodated by tents the Syretts set up near Sunset Point. The couple also fed the group lunch. Later that day, Ruby Syrett brought up five or six beds, which he placed under pine trees near the rim. The Syretts fed the group dinner and breakfast the following morning.

"Whether by design or chance, the Syretts began accommodating tourists," Scrattish pointed out. "They remained near Sunset Point until the fall of that year."

During the spring of 1920, the Syretts decided to build a permanent lodge. The location of that future lodge was on land set aside as a school section by the state, so Mr. Syrett received verbal permission from the State Land Board to erect the structure. That lodge, known as "Tourist's Rest," measured thirty feet by seventy-one feet and was fashioned of sawed logs and included a dining room with a fireplace, a kitchen, a storeroom, and several bedrooms.

"In keeping with the Syrett's informal nature, the lodge's

double front doors served as a guest register," Scrattish wrote. "Visitors thoroughly enjoyed carving their names onto the doors."

The Syretts added eight to ten cabins near the lodge as well as an open-air dance platform. They operated this lodge until it was sold to the Utah Parks Company in 1923 (and a few years later became part of the new park) after which they moved their operation, which they called Ruby's Inn, to where it stands now, just north of the park's main entrance.

The Utah Parks Company built Bryce Lodge a few years later.

Utah Parks Company

The Utah Parks Company, a subsidiary of the Union Pacific Railroad, was the park's main concessionaire in its early years. The company transported its guests via a spur off the main line that reached Cedar City and packed them into twelve-passenger buses for Grand Circle tours to Zion, the North Rim, Bryce Canyon, and Cedar Breaks, with lodges in all four places.

The Parks Company provided special programs for tourists each night and "wild tales to entertain everyone along the way," said Fred Fagergren, who served as Bryce Canyon's super-intendent from 1991-2002.

"This was the first effort to promote these parks and represents what would come as Utah began their Big 5 advertisement efforts," Fagergren explained.

The Grand Circle tour, back in its heyday in the 1920s and 1930s, must have been quite a trip for these early park tourists, according to Fagergren:

> *"When I think of the condition of the roads, the vehicles in which the early visitors rode, the time it would have taken to drive between each of these parks in those slow, pre-air-conditioned buses – the experiences along the roads would have been in stark contrast to the positive experiences once people got to the parks."*

Despite the sometimes rough-going on those Grand Circle tours, the Utah Parks Company created an amicable atmosphere with most of its employees being locals who really valued the places where they worked.

Fun Historic Stops in Southern Utah

"Those connections between local people and the National Parks formed positive bonds and strong friendships that continue to provide support for the National Parks and the environment for years to come," Fagergren said. "Something that has largely disappeared today, except to the extent the parks provide economic support for the local and state economies."

Even though the Utah Parks Company advocated for good roads for its Grand Circle tours, it was those roads, in part, that signaled its demise. By the late 1940s, ridership on those tours had significantly declined, and later, they were discontinued. In 1971, the Utah Parks Company dissolved, and a new concessionaire took its place.

National Park Status

Utah Senator Reed Smoot became a huge proponent of turning Bryce Canyon into a national park. His first attempt came in November 1919, but in the spring of 1920, the Secretary of the Interior reported that it would be more appropriate to designate it as a national monument by presidential proclamation rather than getting Congress involved to make it a national park.

The strong recommendations from the departments of Interior and Agriculture resulted in President William G. Harding pronouncing Bryce Canyon as a national monument on June 8, 1923.

During this time period, the park gained a powerful Eastern ally in Michigan Congressman Louis B. Cramton, who was the chairman of the subcommittee for the Department of Interior appropriations. Cramton had traveled the area extensively and gave a speech to the American Automobile Association, lauding the area's scenic wonders.

As a national monument, the Forest Service administered Bryce Canyon from 1923 to 1928. The Forest Service's major contribution to the monument during its brief tenure as its manager was the construction of good roads to and within the monument, as well as a campground. Stephen Mather, the first NPS director thought that since Utah already had a national park, it didn't need another one.

"He was convinced to come to Utah, and there was a concerted effort to convince him that Bryce Canyon should have another National Park," Fagergren said. "I understand even the LDS church participated in this effort, and a number of young women came down as part of that effort."

Besides the attitude of the Park Service director, there were three other major challenges to overcome before it could become a national park. Number one, all the land within its proposed boundaries needed to be owned by the federal government, which required the state to relinquish some of its land within the park as well as the Union Pacific to deed land it owned to the federal government. Number two, the Zion-Mt. Carmel Highway had to be approved, which would provide better access from Zion to Bryce Canyon. Cramton, in his powerful position, would not approve the road unless the terms creating the national park were also approved. The Union Pacific refused to deed its land until the road was approved as well.

Number three was a naming issue. The original bill enacted to turn it into a national park named it "Utah National Park," which was determined to be too nondescript and was, of course, ultimately scrapped in favor of the name that had stuck since the 1880s. The state only agreed to relinquish its land within the park if the Bryce Canyon name was retained.

On February 25, 1928, Bryce Canyon officially became a national park, but for the first twenty-eight years of its existence, Bryce Canyon was managed by Zion National Park. The NPS justified this choice because, at the time, the park was a seasonal park, open six to eight months a year.

"When the Forest Service tended the monument, visitation in the winter was so slight a snow removal program for existing roads and footpaths was discouraged," Scrattish wrote. "The National Park Service expected this trend to continue, making the need for a separate administration in Bryce Canyon all the more difficult to justify."

For the first few years, the park only had one ranger on duty, Maurice Cope. First employed by the Utah Parks Company to assist tourists at Bryce Canyon Lodge, the NPS hired Cope from May to September starting in 1929. At first, he lived in nearby

Tropic and taught school the rest of the year but moved his family to the park in 1931.

Cope became an integral part of the park's early development.

"I helped to lay out all the trails and roads in the canyon and along the rim," Cope wrote, as quoted in Scrattish's history. "We started to hire help to build trails and make ready to build campgrounds, restrooms, chop wood and haul it for the campers, assign the rangers to the checking station, help patrol, look out for those who might violate the rules, look out for forest fires and anything else that needed attention."

Cope served as a ranger in Bryce Canyon until he transferred to Zion in 1943.

It was during his tenure that local civic pressure to administer the park separate from Zion started at a meeting of the "Associated Civic Clubs of Southern Utah" in November 1934. The NPS still maintained that a joint administration to pool equipment, supplies, and personnel was essential with the limited operating expenses. Not surprisingly, visitation skyrocketed after World War II, and many parks across the country, including Bryce Canyon, were not adequately prepared to handle such crowds and were overrun.

During the summer of 1955, the *Salt Lake Tribune* sought to make its readers aware of the deplorable conditions found in Utah's national parks and monuments through a series of articles. *Tribune* staff writer Don Howard devoted the second article to Bryce Canyon and interviewed Assistant Superintendent Tom Kennedy, who told Howard the park needed more parking space, more scenic viewpoints, more miles of trails and roads, more campsites, and a better museum, as well as better information and interpretive services. Joint administration with Zion had done little to improve things.

Thankfully, National Park Service Director Conrad Wirth launched the "Mission 66" to help the parks to better accommodate their growing visitation by the 50th anniversary of the agency's founding in 1966. The program infused much-needed capital into the National Park Service and did much to improve or replace park facilities around the country and improved morale within the agency's employees. It was a significant reason for the split in park management between Bryce Canyon and Zion, which became official on July 1, 1956.

The change meant the addition of new park staff, including a chief park ranger, chief park naturalist, and an additional park ranger. The Mission 66 program also brought a new visitor center, more employee housing, a modern maintenance yard, and upgrades to its campground.

The Navajo Loop Trail, with its set of numerous switchbacks, is one of the most popular ways for Bryce Canyon visitors to descend below its rim

Ruby's Inn Today

Nearly one hundred years since Ruby and Minnie Syrett first hosted guests in their "Tourist's Rest" along the rim, their location just north of the entrance to the park is still owned by their grandchildren with day-to-day operations managed by their great-grandchildren.

The Inn operated independently until the 1970s when it became affiliated with Best Western. In 1984, the original lodge burned down, unfortunately, but a new one was erected only a year later, said Jean Seiler, Ruby's Inn Marketing Director. The Western town across the highway from Ruby's Inn was added in 1987.

In 2000, the Syrett family developed Bryce View Lodge for budget travelers and eight years later built the Bryce Canyon Grand Hotel for luxury travelers. That same year Ebenezer's Bar and Grill went up, which has become an entertainment and banquet facility. At first, Ebenezer's hosted a cowboy western show but has since transitioned into a country music show with artists from Nashville, Seiler said.

In 2007, the Ruby's Inn area was incorporated as Bryce Canyon City, which raised the ire of Garfield County and its commissioners because of the tax revenue the county would lose with the change since Ruby's Inn is the county's largest employer. There were accusations that the Syrett family was doing it out of greed and a story in the *New York Times* even called Bryce Canyon City a "company town."

However, Seiler said the antagonism toward the incorporation simmered down fast as Garfield County adjusted its tax levy to make up the difference in lost tax revenue.

According to Seiler, Ruby's Inn's motives for incorporating as a town were pure. Until the complex became a city, it was hard to work with government agencies as a private business, he said.

"Now we can cooperate better together," Seiler said. "Now, we're a gateway town, not a gateway business."

Seiler said they ensured that Bryce Canyon City and Ruby's Inn were completely separate entities from the beginning. Two things Bryce Canyon City has done to help both local residents and tourists alike are developing a Public Safety facility and a staging area for the Bryce Canyon Shuttle.

A guided horseback trip traverses the Queen's Garden Trail below the rim of the Bryce Amphitheater with the Sinking Ship formation in the background

Bryce Canyon Today

Transportation is one facet of Bryce's history that has influenced it the most and carries some of the most significant ramifications today, Bryce Canyon Visual Information Specialist Peter Densmore said.

The Utah Parks Company's idea of Grand Circle tours still defines the experience for many travelers today. There is a high probability that visitors who stop at Bryce Canyon will do the same at Zion, the Grand Canyon, and Cedar Breaks Densmore noted.

Today, both Fagergren and Densmore said national parks Bryce Canyon included, are coming full circle and realizing that they need to look at other transportation options to accommodate the growing number of visitors. It's time for Americans to reexamine their relationship with their cars, Densmore said.

Thankfully, Densmore said the public attitude to mass transportation is changing—the younger generation almost expects it. However, some of the older generation, he noted, come in their large RVs and are more reluctant to leave their cars behind because automobiles were heavily marketed in their day and age, and they cannot shake their love affair with their private car.

In 2000, Bryce Canyon initiated a voluntary shuttle system the same year Zion implemented its mandatory shuttle. Fagergren, who was superintendent at the time the shuttle started, said it was a "pretty daring move."

"Unlike Zion, there was no special federal funding to buy buses or any of the other aspects," Fagergren explained. "We sold the idea to D.C. on the concept that Bryce Canyon was the opportunity to test an idea we thought would work and which would encourage visitors to use the shuttle and reduce the number of cars coming into the park."

Even though the shuttle is still going strong today, one of the initial concepts initiated at its inception failed miserably. The park tried to implement what today would be referred to as "congestion pricing," in which visitors paid a higher fee to enter the park if they drove their cars in, but those riding the shuttle would pay a lower fee.

"Unfortunately, that concept lasted one day," Fagergren said. "There were so many complaints that went all the way to the top in Washington, D.C. that we deserted the two-fee concept."

Currently, the Bryce Canyon shuttle, which stops at the major staging areas along the rim of the main amphitheater, only operates from April through October, but Densmore said, like the Zion Shuttle, the season continues to expand. For instance, the park has extended the shuttle's season by a month as a result of the uptick in visitation.

The park saw 2,679,478 visitors in 2018, which was up by 107,794 visits from the year before, and up over 1.6 million visits from 2010. Even though Bryce Canyon's shuttle is voluntary, it still has been vital in dealing with the park's visitor congestion, Densmore said. The reception to the shuttle is generally positive, with many visitors preferring to leave their cars parked and board the bus.

Like many parks, Bryce Canyon is at a crossroads as to what to do to accommodate the rising number of visitors. One of the options is to expand the shuttles' capacity and routes and possibly make it mandatory, Densmore explained, which doesn't seem as if it would cause much of a ripple because after visiting Zion, many visitors expect the shuttle to be mandatory.

Bryce Canyon has more challenges than just increasing visitation, however, including infrastructure needs, housing for seasonal workers, deferred maintenance, visitor communication, fire suppression, and inadequate staffing. The Bryce Canyon Natural History Association, the official nonprofit partner of the park, has been a vital partner for the park to help fill its funding gaps.

"We would be in a completely different situation without that partnership," Densmore said.

The BCNHA has provided over nine million to help the park and has worked with Ruby's Inn and Bryce Canyon Lodge to help fundraise for the park. The program allows visitors to add one dollar to the price of each night's stay that goes directly to the Association to fund some of the park's needs that are not covered by its annual budget.

Park management will continue to change things up to meet the park's challenges.

The erosive forces of wind, water, and ice that carved the hoodoos of the amphitheater will continue to change as well. For instance, the Sentinel, along the Navajo Trail near Thor's Hammer, succumbed to that erosion in December 2016. It won't be the last.

Visiting Bryce Canyon

There are plenty of activities to do in Bryce Canyon, chief among them is hiking its many trails, including a stroll along the rim of the main amphitheater. However, to truly appreciate its many hoodoos, it is essential to descend below the rim on trails such as Navajo Loop, Queen's Garden, and Peek-a-boo Loop.

The busiest tourist area is along the rim of the main amphitheater between Bryce Canyon Lodge and Bryce Point. To see fewer crowds, visitors can hike the Fairyland Loop, whose trailhead is near the north entrance, or head farther south along the road and check out the viewpoints south of the main amphitheater, such as Swamp Canyon, Ponderosa Canyon, Natural Bridge, and the two southernmost views of the park, Rainbow and Yovimpa points.

The original story and photo gallery can be found at the following link:

https://www.stgeorgeutah.com/news/archive/2019/05/19/raw-bryce-canyon-day-a-grand-erosive-spectacle-with-an-identity-crisis/

FOR FURTHER INFORMATION
Bryce Canyon National Park website

https://www.nps.gov/brca/index.htm

*An old-fashioned manure spreader stands next
to the recently restored Butch Cassidy Boyhood Home
south of Circleville, Utah*

4

BUTCH CASSIDY BOYHOOD HOME
The Notorious Outlaw's Legacy, Both Real and Imagined, Restored in Circleville

One would think that a historical figure who still casts a wide shadow more than one hundred years after his death would be someone whose actions in life exuded the true definition of heroism—a military commander, a civil rights activist, or president.

A notorious outlaw certainly doesn't fit the definition of a true hero, but one particular son of Mormon pioneers who settled in Southern Utah is a bandit anomaly—both in his "real" and "reel" personas.

In his "real" life, Butch Cassidy was not a cold-blooded, ruthless killer in the mold of Jesse James or Billy the Kid. While he always wielded a gun, he didn't use one much. As far as historians have pieced together, he never shot and killed anyone, and if he would have had to shoot, it would have been in self-defense.

He was calm, collected, and calculating, which is what endeared him to others and attracted outlaws to be part of his gang, "The Wild Bunch." His robberies were not spur-of-the-moment, haphazard affairs, but carefully planned weeks and even months in advance. He staked out his targets to discover their nuances, especially the best time to strike. He set fresh relay horses along his escape routes, so posses would hardly have a chance in their pursuit.

Cassidy was respectful to women and gave back to the less fortunate. Even lawmen described him as gentlemanly, and he kept his promises to them. For instance, when he was released from the Wyoming State Penitentiary for horse thievery—the only time he ever spent in "the pen"—he promised his captors he would never steal another horse in the state and was true to his word (though he did later rob trains in the state).

In his "reel" life, as played by Paul Newman in the 1969 film *Butch Cassidy and the Sundance Kid*, he was just as charming, and he had a way with people that was lacking in the Sundance Kid—played by Robert Redford. Screenwriter William Goldman's witty dialogue tremendously aided his "reel" persona, making it stand out from the screenplays of many other by-the-book Westerns.

Butch Cassidy and the Sundance Kid was the antithesis of the normal formulaic Western in another way: The protagonists are actually the "bad" guys and the ones being chased instead of doing the chasing.

The movie helped increase interest in the beloved bandit and perpetuate the legends surrounding his real life and questions surrounding his death. The movie's ending, the duo's 1908 shoot-out with Bolivian troops (after living in South America for nearly seven years when things got too hot in the United States), is ambiguous and leaves it up to the audience to decide whether the two outlaws really met their demise in that confrontation.

Many are sure the 1908 shootout in Bolivia was the end for Cassidy, but his family and old-timers who knew him—as well as a whole host of Butch Cassidy aficionados—say otherwise. Lula Parker Betenson, Cassidy's sister, wrote a book entitled *Butch Cassidy, My Brother* in 1975, in which she recounts when she saw him at a family gathering in 1925. Betenson says the exact date when he died and where he is buried is a closely-guarded family secret.

In 2012, Lula Betenson's great-grandson, Bill Betenson, published *Butch Cassidy, My Uncle: A Family Portrait* after over twenty years of research. The main purpose of his book is to dispel rumors and provide background on his family. Both he and his great grandmother claim none of the family members or old-timers who identified Cassidy at that family gathering had anything to gain by telling such tales. He also noted that his great grandmother would have been taken more seriously as a woman in her forties dressed in a business suit than an octogenarian assumed to have succumbed to senility.

Larry Pointer's *In Search of Butch Cassidy*, originally published in 1977, presented the story of a Spokane man named William T. Phillips presumed to be Butch Cassidy. Phillips authored a manuscript entitled "The Bandit Invincible," which Pointer said bore a strong resemblance to the exploits of Butch Cassidy and recounted information only Cassidy would know. After Phillips' death in 1937, his widow denied that her husband was the actual Butch Cassidy, but simply said Phillips knew Cassidy well.

Phillips' widow was right on both accounts. As described in an August 2011 *Deseret News* article by Michael De Groote, Pointer came across a longer version of the manuscript Phillips wrote, and through research prompted by the second manuscript, Pointer found that Phillips was an outlaw contemporary of Cassidy's whose real name was William T. Wilcox. Wilcox and Cassidy served time together in the Wyoming State Penitentiary, and both went to Lander, Wyoming, after being released from prison only about a month apart.

For Pointer, who was the biggest believer in his circumstantial-evidence story of Phillips as the real Cassidy, the new revelation was hard to take, but he admitted he could deny it no longer. However, the Bolivian shootout story was also dealt a blow when the two bodies that were supposedly those of Butch and Sundance were exhumed and DNA tested in the early 1990s. The DNA did not match.

But such stories are what makes the legend of Butch Cassidy so much fun and why so many cannot resist it. Historians even dispute which robberies Cassidy and his gang participated in. Pointer theorized in the epilogue of his book that there could have been multiple Butch Cassidys and that some members of Butch's family turned out to be smaller-scale outlaws, including his brother, Dan, whom Bill Betenson talks about in depth in his book.

But the myths about Butch Cassidy aren't anything new. They started during his lifetime.

For instance, in November 1901, *The Salt Lake Tribune* reported the following:

> *"Butch Cassidy has more lives than a dozen cats, and his ubiquitousness is more than a match for his multitudinous lives. He has been killed time and again within the past five years, and he has also taken part in every notorious robbery during that time. Butch Cassidy is not a mere man; he is a criminal syndicate."*

Butch Cassidy's Footprint

The Butch Cassidy 5K/10K race in early November, sponsored by Springdale and Rockville, celebrates the haunts of the "reel" Butch Cassidy, with Grafton ghost town being its main focus and the race's finish line.

During movie filming in the fall of 1968, Twentieth Century-Fox built a frame home in Grafton on a corner across the street from the old schoolhouse/church as the home of Etta Place, the Sundance Kid's love interest. Grafton was the backdrop of one of the most iconic scenes of the movie, when Katherine Ross, as Etta Place, rides on the handlebars of a bike while Newman, as Cassidy, pedals through the town to the sound of "Raindrops Keep Falling on My Head."

Cave Valley in Zion National Park's Kolob Terrace section also served as the Wild Bunch's hideout and parts of Zion and Snow Canyon State Park hosted chase scenes.

However, the "real" Butch Cassidy spent much more time farther north, most prominently in Beaver, where he was born Robert LeRoy Parker on April 13, 1866, and in Circleville, where he lived as a teenager from approximately 1880-1884. It was from Circleville that he left to begin his life of crime after falling in with the wrong crowd, especially a horse rustler by the name of Mike Cassidy, whose last name he took to protect his real family name.

A sign along the highway states all of the organizations that helped make the restoration of the Butch Cassidy Boyhood Home a reality

Boyhood Home Restoration

Circleville, in southernmost Piute County, is the Butch Cassidy capital of Utah. This designation was recently enhanced with the restoration of Cassidy's boyhood home, which actually sits approximately a mile south of Circleville just over the Garfield County line.

For decades, the home sat literally rotting from the bottom up. It is located on private land owned by Afton Morgan in the middle of an actively farmed hay field. The Morgan family wanted the cabin and site preserved, as did the two counties, but none of them had the resources to do it.

Piute County Commissioner Darin Bushman stepped in and became the project's champion and catalyst, wanting to preserve the historical relic and also augment tourism in his county. Garfield County became a vital part of the team, as well.

The restoration process started in 2014 when a National Park Service archeology architect provided a glimpse of what it would need, which was mainly a foundation. The architect determined that if they really wanted to preserve the cabin, they would have to take it apart and put it back together on a new foundation.

"That was a little more than we could bite off," Bushman said.

The next step was going to Savage Albrecht Engineering to get an estimate of the cost, which turned out to be $350,000.

After obtaining that figure, fundraising began.

They also turned to Fred Hayes, Director of the Utah Division of Parks and Recreation, which administers the state parks and also manages the state's off-highway vehicle program. The cabin site sits very near the well-known Paiute ATV Trail, so with the help of Senator Ralph Okerlund, the Utah Legislature appropriated $138,000 from the off-highway vehicle restricted fund to help with the stabilization and restoration of the cabin. As part of the restoration, the trail was extended to reach the cabin, Bushman said.

Another $50,000 for the restoration came from the Utah Heritage Highway 89 Alliance and $11,000 from the Paiute Trail Committee, Bushman said. Much of the rest of the project was done through donated materials and volunteer labor, including the two counties coming together to do the dirty work for the approach to the cabin and the parking lot, Bushman said. Volunteer laborers also completed all of the fencing.

The cabin now serves as a trailside attraction and a stopover for travelers on U.S. Highway 89.

"Now think about that for a minute," Hayes said. "Two counties, the state, and a private family coming together for a really cool project. That kind of cooperation is the 'Utah way' of making things happen."

Even though the cabin has no ties to a state park, the Division of Parks and Recreation has had a hand in it because it has been tasked with assisting historic preservation within the state, especially when such a project will help the area's economy, Hayes said.

Piute County, statistically, has the weakest economy in the state. Bushman described how it has suffered from what can be considered the "Route 66 effect." When a bigger, better thoroughfare comes through, the towns along the formerly busy highway suffer, which is just what happened when I-70 connected to I-15. Even today, Bushman said that if someone coming from Colorado, for example, were to get directions from Google maps to Bryce Canyon, it would route them away from Piute County.

Bushman said he sees the boyhood home as an asset to attract more people to the county. Today, signs near Exit 23 of I-70—the intersection with Highway 89—direct potential travelers off the freeway to the restored cabin. Other signage along Highway 89 alerts motorists that the home is coming up.

At the dedication of the restored home on September 19, 2017, Hayes said, "Everyone had a story"—mainly of when ancestors helped out Butch Cassidy or interacted with him.

"The dedication was a big deal," Bushman said.

He didn't know just how big it would be and wished he would have brought in more bleachers for the ceremony. Besides locals, there were even people in attendance from Colorado, Idaho, Montana, and Wyoming—all because they are keenly interested in Butch Cassidy.

The Piute County Rodeo royalty and entire student body of Circleville Elementary took part in the ceremony, as well as Clive Romney from Utah Pioneer Heritage Arts, who provided entertainment, including Butch Cassidy songs and poems.

Bushman said that even as he and fellow project participants sat on the picnic table on the site, the highway noise disappeared, adding that he has heard owner Afton Morgan call it: "The most peaceful place on the planet."

To many, the restored Cassidy boyhood home might just seem like another run-of-the-mill historic cabin. But it's not. There is definitely a different aura there.

"As you stand there," Hayes said, "you can feel the history. It's an important site."

A mile north of the cabin is Butch Cassidy's Hideout Cafe and Motel, the de facto Butch Cassidy Visitor Center. Practically daily, diners come into the eatery seeking information about Cassidy, and owners Mike and Kelli Cummings and their staff are happy to answer visitors' questions, usually directing them to the cabin south of town.

"They stop because of the name and because they're curious," said Kelli Cummings, who also serves on the county tourism board.

She said she regularly sees people from other countries stopping in and that because of Cassidy's English ancestry, he's also celebrated in the United Kingdom.

Cummings said that about fifty percent of the economy in southern Piute County comes from Butch Cassidy tourism, adding that she needs to start counting the number of tourists who are "In Search of Butch Cassidy," just like the title of Pointer's book.

Red Canyon boasts a trail named after Butch Cassidy

Visiting Butch Cassidy's Footprint in South-Central Utah

While Circleville is ground zero for Butch Cassidy lore, there are many other places one can visit in the region to get a piece of Butch Cassidy history–real or imagined–and view landmarks named after Cassidy. Below is a list (by no means exhaustive) of a few places to visit besides his boyhood home:

Cassidy Arch, Capitol Reef National Park – While there is no evidence Cassidy even ventured near the arch, it is named after the outlaw, perhaps because of its proximity to Robbers' Roost, a popular hideout of the Wild Bunch, listed below.

Old Pine Inn, Marysvale, Utah – This is another spot in Piute County where Butch Cassidy purportedly spent some time. The Old Pine Inn claims to be the longest-running hotel within the state (established in 1882) during his outlaw career.

Red Canyon – Allegedly, Cassidy got into a brawl over a girl at a dance in Panguitch and made his escape via Red Canyon, full of crimson-hued hoodoos similar to those in Bryce Canyon National Park. Some parts of that escape route are said to be included in the Cassidy Trail, whose trailhead is near SR-12's mile marker 4.

Robbers Roost, East of Hanksville, Utah – Given its remoteness and unforgiving terrain, this area was a popular hideout for Cassidy and his Wild Bunch because lawmen dared not penetrate it.

Western Mining and Railroad Museum, Helper, Utah – This museum boasts a few steps from the Pleasant Valley Coal Company office, which Cassidy and his gang robbed of approximately $7,000 in gold on April 22, 1897. The robbery is the only one attributed to Cassidy within the state of Utah, and in typical Cassidy style, he cut telegraph lines before the robbery so authorities could not be alerted easily and retreated to Robber's Roost.

Fun Historic Stops in Southern Utah

Author's Note: *This story was originally published on November 5, 2017. Since then, Fred Hayes, the Director of the Utah Division of Parks and Recreation quoted in the story, has passed away.*

The original story and photo gallery can be found at the following link:

https://www.stgeorgeutah.com/news/
archive/2017/11/05/butch-cassidy-day-the-
notorious-outlaws-legacy-both-real-and-
imagined-restored-in-circleville/

FOR FURTHER INFORMATION
Butch Cassidy Boyhood Home Facebook Page:

https://www.facebook.com/ButchCassidy
Home/

The sun sets aglow the Cedar Breaks amphitheater of multicolored hoodoos | photo courtesy of Mike Saemisch

5

CEDAR BREAKS

How an Early Rivalry Set the Stage For the 'Crown Jewel of the Markagunt Plateau'

While Cedar Breaks National Monument may sport magnificent views of spires and hoodoos reminiscent of Bryce Canyon ranging in color from white to red, education was actually one of the main reasons for the park's establishment, and it is still central to its mission today.

The park, which sits above 10,000 feet approximately twenty miles east of Cedar City, is the crown jewel of the Markagunt Plateau. In archaic days, it was the domain of early people down to the Paiutes, who migrated to and from the plateau with the weather. Settlers–sheepherders, dairymen, and ranchers–discovered it in 1868, describing it as "a paradise on the mountain," according to one early scout.

That paradise eventually became part of the climax of the National Park Service's early rivalry with the U.S. Forest Service.

Fun Historic Stops in Southern Utah

In a 1987 article in the Utah State Historical Quarterly entitled "The Cedar Breaks Proposal," late UNLV history professor Hal Rothman reported that the Forest Service felt slighted because it believed too much of its land was being transferred to National Park Service jurisdiction and that if it kept happening it would threaten the Forest Service's very existence.

Cedar Breaks was on the radar of Stephen Mather, the park service's first director, since the early 1920s, Rothman wrote. Mather hoped to add it to the agency's Southern Utah portfolio as part of loop tours through the other parks in the area. However, Mather's successor, Horace Albright, vociferously campaigned for its designation as a national park, initially planning to add it as a satellite section of Zion or Bryce Canyon national parks.

If it had been up to a group of Salt Lake City businessmen, Cedar Breaks and Bryce Canyon would have been part of a large, contiguous Zion National Park, said Dale Topham, a history instructor at Brookhaven College in Texas who wrote a followup article to Rothman's in the Summer 2017 issue of UHQ.

At first, Albright met strong resistance from the Forest Service, local ranching interests, then Utah Senator William King (Utah's other senator at the time, Reed Smoot, supported it) and even a few within his own agency, but he would not give up.

To get the monument approved, Albright relented on its size, only choosing the area having the most scenic merit. After receiving a proposal from the Forest Service's Chief Forester, Robert Stuart, to keep it under that agency's auspices and offer the same type of services the park service provided, including education, Albright saw his opening, Rothman reported.

In a letter to Stuart dated April 4, 1933, Albright wrote:

"If the Cedar Breaks area is most valuable to the public because of timber or grazing resources, administration would naturally come under the Forest Service. However, this area is scenic rather than industrially useful . . . and the public (should be) afforded a unified educational service such as the Park Service is equipped to supply."

Early tourists felt the same way.

In the 1920s, the Utah Parks Company, a subsidiary of the Union Pacific that led national park tours and administered prime lodging in Zion, Bryce Canyon, and the Grand Canyon's North Rim, started leading tours that included the three parks. Cedar Breaks was included on some of those tours.

Visitors noticed that the experience was different at Cedar Breaks because it was under Forest Service jurisdiction at the time. They came expecting the same educational experience they had received at the other parks but didn't get it.

"The National Park Service was set up to provide education, the Forest Service was not," said Josh LaMore, an intern at Cedar Breaks, who has done extensive research on the monument's history and wrote the book *Beauty Beyond Telling*, about the monument.

The park service's ability to provide education became the avenue Albright needed to establish the monument. Rothman reports that even Stuart himself could not refute Albright's argument and agreed to transfer the monument, which paved the way for the Franklin D. Roosevelt administration to designate it a national monument on August 22, 1933.

A ceremony commemorating the monument's creation took place on July 4, 1934, and was the first time Civilian Conservation Corps enrollees made an appearance in the monument. CCC boys directed traffic, assisted drivers with stalled cars, and served a barbecue dinner at the event, LaMore said.

The CCC had a lasting impact on Cedar Breaks. The Corps was responsible for building the visitor center as well as the caretaker's cabin in 1937. The visitor center, built in the rustic style popular at the time and designed to blend into the park environment, is one of the few CCC-built visitor centers still in use today within the National Park Service system, LaMore said.

The story of lodging in the monument is both interesting and sometimes contentious.

From 1921 to approximately 1926, a building affectionately known as Minnie's Mansion, located on what is now the monument's north end and built by one of Brian Head's original homesteading families, the Adamses, played host to many dairy and sheepherding families as a place to eat, lodge, and even dance the night away. It also became a popular place to go for the Fourth of July, LaMore said—a tradition that the town of Brian Head has kept going to this day. Sadly, the season was too short to turn a profit, and its heyday was short-lived. Today, small pieces of its foundation and shards of its window glass are all that remain.

In 1924, the Utah Parks Company built the Cedar Breaks Lodge to accommodate tourists enjoying its Grand Circle National Park bus tours. Designed by renowned architect Gilbert Stanley Underwood, it was the smallest of the four lodges the UPC constructed. The UPC tour buses often stopped at Cedar Breaks Lodge for dinner before returning to Cedar City's train depot.

"A dollar twenty-five bought a chicken dinner, complete with mashed potatoes, gravy, homemade bread, and dessert," one NPS Cedar Breaks history page states. "The Lodge seated one hundred twenty people—some nights the tables were set three times to accommodate tour buses and locals who had come up to spend the evening."

The 1920s were the heyday of the Utah Parks Company. As passenger service on the railroads declined, more tourists arrived via private automobile, slowly signaling the death knell of the subsidiary, which held on until the late 1960s in Cedar Breaks. Forced to complete costly improvements on Cedar Breaks Lodge to renew its concessionaire contract in 1968, the UPC discontinued service in Cedar Breaks, but TWA Recreational Services took over its operations in the other three parks.

UPC donated the Lodge to the park service in 1971.

"They handed it all over and said, 'Good luck,'" LaMore said.

The building and its outlying cabins were offered to various institutions "as a National Outdoor Environmental Study Area," LaMore wrote in an article prepared for the park service about the lodge's demise. All of the organizations declined, and the buildings were put up for auction in 1972. Only three bidders showed up for the auction, and the winning bidder ended up paying one dollar each for the cabins, which were hauled out intact on flatbed trailers. However, none of the bidders bid on the lodge. Some suggest that no one wanted the lodge because of the expensive upgrades for which the park service was asking, Lamore said, and that led to the building's dismantling and removal.

"There has been lots of talk about parts and pieces of the Cedar Breaks Lodge existing in various locations of southern Utah," LaMore wrote in the article. "The good news is that these rumors are more than likely true."

Many locals were not happy about the lodge's demise, LaMore said, but there was a silver lining.

"As sad and disappointing as the removal of Cedar Breaks Lodge is," LaMore wrote, "it's important to remember that its removal brought forth such an outcry from the local communities that the Zion Lodge and Bryce Canyon Lodge were saved from a similar fate."

In more recent history, attempts have been made to fulfill Albright's original vision for Cedar Breaks—to make it a national park. The proposals have garnered a lot of local support, but have never gotten over the hump. One proposal included expanding the park to take in Ashdown Gorge Wilderness Area and Flanigan Arch, Ken Watson, Cedar Breaks Chief of Interpretation, said.

Even to this day, the thought to elevate the monument's status has not died. There is talk of trying it again, Watson said, but nothing has materialized.

The Zion National Park Forever Project, a recently reorganized nonprofit partner of Zion National Park and Cedar Breaks and Pipe Spring national monuments, will be a boon to Cedar Breaks, Watson said. One hundred percent of entrance fees stay within the monument, but they're not enough to truly make the park great, and that's where the Forever Project comes in.

"It's going to prop up those extra things," Watson said of the nonprofit's funding, which will help bolster outreach programs and other worthy causes at the park.

Current funding priorities the Zion Forever Project is working on for Cedar Breaks are for preserving Southern Utah's dark skies, establishing a citizen science monitoring program, preparing a design and site plan for an education center, curating an oral history project, and establishing a Cedar Breaks-to-Brian Head trail network. The park itself boasts four trails, ranging from the easy, short, paved Campground and Sunset trails to the Spectra Point/Ramparts Overlook Trail that traverses the rim with more elevation gain.

Visiting Cedar Breaks in the winter provides rewarding views of snow-covered hoodoos and winter recreation opportunities such as snowshoeing and cross-country skiing | photo courtesy of Mike Saemisch

Visiting Cedar Breaks

July and August are a particularly good time to visit Cedar Breaks as the weather is ideal, and the park offers many summer events, including the Chasing Light Plein Air Art Festival and Wildflower Festival. Just like the days of yore, Cedar Breaks offers its modern-day visitors a plethora of educational opportunities, including summer and winter star parties and wintertime guided snowshoe excursions. Many of these events are seeing full attendance.

Proud of its designation as an International Dark Sky Park, Cedar Breaks has ramped up astronomy programs recently.

"We want to make astronomy accessible," Watson said.

The weekly summer star parties provide visitors a chance to learn about the importance of dark night skies, go on a constellation tour and view celestial bodies such as the moon, star clusters, nebulae, and other galaxies through telescopes. The monument also hosts an astronomy festival in the fall.

In addition to its remarkable scenery and a spate of summer activities, because of its high altitude, Cedar Breaks offers a welcome respite from the summer heat permeating the Southern Utah regions below.

The original story and photo gallery can be found at the following link:

https://www.stgeorgeutah.com/news/
archive/2018/09/09/dsr-raw-cedar-breaks-
day-how-early-rivalry-set-the-stage-for-the-
crown-jewel-of-the-markagunt-plateau/

FOR FURTHER INFORMATION
Cedar Breaks National Monument website:

https://www.nps.gov/cebr/planyourvisit/
index.htm

Duck Creek flows below Aspen Mirror Lake, a popular fishing spot just west of Duck Creek Village

6

DUCK CREEK VILLAGE
First a "Movie Ranch," Now an ATV Haven

Benefiting from its location close to red rock country, Duck Creek Village's meadows and surrounding aspen, fir and pine forests served as a stand-in for several other places, including New York and Kentucky, which might be a little bit of a stretch, as well as Wyoming, which is not so much of a stretch.

The mountain resort hamlet located on Cedar Mountain in northwestern Kane County along State Route 14 was lucky enough to be an extension of "Little Hollywood" during nearby Kanab's western moviemaking heyday.

It was known as "Movie Ranch," a moniker proudly displayed on its street signs today.

Interpretive signs at Duck Creek Visitor Center explain the

area's earliest history, calling it its "explosive past" because of the involvement of volcanoes in forming cinder cones, which became the natural dam that impounded nearby Navajo Lake and the black lava beds so prominent in the area that looks like a fleet of dump trucks just left them there. In actuality, they formed when hot magma oozed out of the bases of gassy cinder cones like a river and covered the surrounding land.

Paiutes and their ancestors roamed the land for centuries, and once the white man made his debut in the area, just like many of the scenic and recreational destinations on Cedar Mountain, such as Cedar Breaks, Duck Creek became the domain of sheepherders; in fact, it was a favorite gathering place for them.

In the 1930s, the Civilian Conservation Corps played a role in Duck Creek's early development with its Duck Creek Recreation Camp, which was dedicated on June 25, 1933, with a keynote address by Utah's then-Governor Henry Blood and performances by a male chorus from Kanab and a band from Parowan.

The *Kane County Standard* called Duck Creek an "ideal place to establish a recreation camp, the air being cool and refreshing, the scenery enchanting and there is good fishing along Duck Creek," Martha Bradley reported in her book about Kane County's history. "There is no doubt but that this camp will become a popular retreat as soon as it is known to all who wish to spend a few days or weeks camping in a shady and quiet place among the pines and aspens."

The CCC work center built at the site included two residences, one office building, one barn, a gas house, and a warehouse. The work center would serve as housing for a Forest Service ranger and some summer employees and was a central point that provided easy access to local recreational areas such as Navajo Lake, Cedar Breaks, Duck Creek, Aspen Mirror Lake, Mammoth Creek, and Strawberry Point.

Local workers were hired to lead the battalion of CCC enrollees, most of whom were from Eastern states. The CCC Camp, known as F-16, spent the summer months first building the work center, then the Duck Creek Campground to the north. Other projects completed by the CCC boys included road construction, the building of a dike across Navajo Lake, and even porcupine eradication.

The CCC camp remained active until the early 1940s when the CCC was disbanded. The work camp office building was renovated in 1994 and now serves as the Duck Creek Forest Service Visitor Center. The other buildings were demolished due to the discovery of radon gas in them.

Some of the best-known movies filmed on location in Duck Creek Village include *Drums Along the Mohawk* (1939) starring Henry Fonda (its turn impersonating New York), *National Velvet* (1944) starring Elizabeth Taylor, *My Friend Flicka* (1943) and its sequel, *Thunderhead, Son of Flicka* (1945), *The Green Grass of Wyoming* (1948), and *Smoky* (1950) starring Fred MacMurray, among others.

During the 1950s and 1960s, visitors were allowed on the movie locations at Duck Creek with the stipulation that they would be quiet during filming, James V. D'Arc notes in his book *When Hollywood Came to Town: A History of Moviemaking in Utah*. Some lucky local visitors to the sets even went home with autographs from their favorite stars.

For instance, ten-year-old Cedar City resident Scott Boyter had the thrill of his life meeting and getting the autograph of one of his heroes, Clint Walker (famous for his role in the television series *Cheyenne*) during the filming of the movie *Fort Dobbs* (1958) in the Duck Creek area. D'Arc's book recounted Boyter's experience in his own words:

> *"I remember going up to Cedar Mountain in our car, and I took my little Browning camera along with me. What is particularly interesting at that time, one could drive right up to the set. It was at Aspen Mirror Lake, right off Route 14. We got out of the car and walked a few steps, and there they were. No one was yelling at us to get out of the way or to be quiet. I quickly took a few pictures when I recognized Clint Walker. You couldn't miss him, as he stood literally head and shoulders above everyone else."*

Boyter drummed up the courage to ask Walker to sign the "Cheyenne" comic book he'd brought at the urging of his mother. When he approached, Walker didn't notice him, and co-star Virginia Mayo had to point him out. Boyter continued to describe his encounter with Walker:

> "He turned around and, in a deep voice, said, 'Yes, son?' I was scared to death and managed to nervously ask, 'Mr. Walker, may I have your autograph, please?' 'Where do you want it, son?' 'Oh, anyplace is fine,' I replied. So, he opened up the comic book and signed his name in pencil, since I did not have a pen with me. 'Is that all right?' he asked. 'Yes,' I said, 'that's just fine."

The 1960s television series *Daniel Boone*, starring Fess Parker, was Duck Creek's turn impersonating Kentucky's backwoods. By the end of the 1960s, Duck Creek's use as a filming location halted, and a new chapter of its history began.

Starting in the 1960s, it became a retreat for second home owners with the Movie Ranch Subdivision and has continued growing and gaining popularity since. Craig Primas, president of the Duck Creek Village Association, said many of its homeowners are from the Las Vegas area or Southern California. Only five to ten percent of homeowners live there full time.

Currently, Duck Creek is trying to make itself more attractive with an improved streetscape, including a boardwalk, better lighting, and more parking. Primas, a retired civil engineer, and current fine-arts photographer, said he would like to make it a place visitors driving by want to stop and explore as well as a better environment for businesses, some of which start and last for two or three years and then close their doors.

Since Duck Creek is an unincorporated area of Kane County, Primas and the association have presented their proposal to the Kane County Commission to garner its support.

"It is the vision of this project that travelers will one day look down from Highway 14 onto the 'postcard' of Duck Creek Village and say 'Look, honey, let's go down there. That is a very cute village,'" Primas and the Duck Creek Village Association wrote in their presentation to the County Commission. "And once there, the travelers, perhaps en route to Bryce Canyon, will stay for a day or even longer, when they find the parking easy, the boardwalk welcoming, the Main Street safe, the shops quaint, and the people friendly."

The Commission is on board and has pledged financial support, but the construction of the improvements might be slow to come to fruition, Primas said. The construction might be done in phases, the first phase being a way to demonstrate the major difference the upgrades will make for the community and help those not fully convinced of what their impact could be.

Duck Creek does a lot for the Kane County economy, Primas said, and he feels it's time for it to receive a little more from the county in return.

The Duck Creek Visitor Center, a renovated Civilian Conservation Corps work camp building, is the best place to start for anyone visiting Duck Creek

Visiting Duck Creek

Duck Creek Village is reached via a twenty-nine-mile scenic drive from Cedar City up SR-14. Its main business district on Movie Ranch Road features eateries, shops, rental cabins, all-terrain vehicle rental locations, and real estate offices.

It boasts miles and miles of ATV/off-highway vehicle trails nearby, making it an ATV/OHV haven in the summertime and an ideal snowmobiling location in the winter.

The area is also a popular fishing spot with Aspen Mirror Lake, Duck Creek Pond, and Navajo Lake all within five miles. Camping options are plentiful at the nearby Duck Creek Campground, Navajo Lake, and other nearby locations.

An excellent place to start a visit to Duck Creek is at the visitor center, located across the highway from Duck Creek Pond and before the highway reaches the main business district.

The visitor center includes a plethora of free pamphlets and brochures about recreation options in the area. Friendly forest rangers and volunteers at the visitor center will be happy to answer questions and provide a list entitled "16 things to do within 16 miles" which includes activities such as hiking the Cascade Falls and Singing Pines trails, exploring three caves—Bower, Ice and Mammoth—and more.

The original story and photo gallery can be found at the following link:

https://www.stgeorgeutah.com/news/archive/2019/07/14/raw-duck-creek-day-a-very-cute-village-first-movie-ranch-now-atv-haven/

FOR FURTHER INFORMATION
Duck Creek Village Visitor Center website:

https://www.fs.usda.gov/recarea/dixie/recarea/?recid=24854

Goblin Valley is an erosive spectacle like no other with rocks that resemble anything one's imagination can dream up

7

GOBLIN VALLEY STATE PARK
A Late-explored, Otherworldly Erosive Spectacle

Many first-time Goblin Valley State Park visitors, upon seeing the state park's vast array of red rock formations, say they feel like they are on another planet. Technically known as hoodoos, the formations resemble anything one's imagination can think up.

"Goblin Valley is filled with stone babies, goblins, ghosts and toadstools that range in height from ten to two hundred feet," said longtime *Salt Lake Tribune* reporter and columnist Tom Wharton in the Utah guide he wrote as part of the "Compass Guides" series. "They stand like families of red goblins poured out, one by one, by a giant wizard and left frozen in time."

Other guests and writers have described it similarly, some comparing it to the surface of Mars.

While not actually off the surface of Earth, Goblin Valley *has* served as a stand-in for another planet in the 1999 *Star Trek* spoof *Galaxy Quest* and as inhospitable terrain in a few other movies.

But the scenic wonderland literally wasn't on the map until 1949.

"Valley of the Mushrooms:" The 1949 Expedition

When one thinks of famous explorers in Utah's history, names such as Dominguez and Escalante, John C. Fremont, Parley P. Pratt, and John Wesley Powell might come to mind, but probably not Arthur Chaffin.

By 1949, one would think Utah would have already been completely explored and mapped, but that wasn't the case. Goblin Valley still remained a mystery. However, when San Francisco resident Philip Tompkins—a land assayer, explorer, and amateur historian—just couldn't get enough of the incredible scenery of the Utah and Arizona deserts, he became the impetus for an exploring expedition into the now-iconic bastion of Utah scenery.

Tompkins made the acquaintance of Chaffin and hired him as his guide, saying he'd like to see some new scenery. Chaffin first came across Goblin Valley on horseback in 1921 while, as Wayne County Commissioner, he was looking for a feasible route for an oiled road between Caineville and Green River. The area had likely been visited previously by Native Americans and cattle ranchers searching for straying steers, but the "discovery" of Goblin Valley is clearly pinned on him.

During that 1921 exploration, Chaffin took notice of the area and marked its location on a rough map that he put in his saddlebags, but he never forgot about the area, trying to no avail to interest his photographer friends to join him in a more thorough exploration.

Chaffin became a pioneer in the tourist trade in southeastern Utah, operating a ferry across the Colorado River at what is now Lake Powell's Hite Marina, all the while continually exploring the land. After Tompkin's request to see something a little different, Chaffin knew he'd found just the person to accompany him back to what he first christened "Valley of the Mushrooms."

"Chaffin reached into his desk drawer, pulled out the map he'd scrawled many years before, and said 'I think we might have something here to fit that bill,'" Barry Scholl wrote in a story about that 1949 expedition in the May/June 1997 issue of *Salt Lake Magazine*.

In September 1949, Chaffin and Tompkins set out with brothers Perry and Worthen Jackson to explore the showcase of red rock curiosities. They rattled over the open desert in a filled-to-the-brim war surplus Jeep with Chaffin alternately leading and riding his horse, Star. Within a mile of reaching their destination, the Jeep became stuck in the desert's deep sand, prompting the men to abandon it and trudge on with Chaffin leading the way atop Star. They reached Goblin Valley's western edge on September 20. Seeing it rendered them speechless. "I thought it was pretty amazing, I'll tell you," Perry Jackson told Scholl in an interview for his story. "None of us except Arthur had seen anything like it before, and even he didn't have anything to say."

Tompkins wrote an article of his impressions of his first visit in a 1954 article for *National Parks Bulletin*.

"The expanse, covered with thousands of sandstone figures, was overwhelming in its effect," Tompkins wrote, adding that it looked like "a huge corral filled with animals."

"At close range, the grotesque figures suggested the name Goblin Valley. That was the name we gave it."

Using "goblin" to describe it is certainly more mysterious and enticing than "mushroom."

Within hours after their arrival, Tompkins could tell he didn't have enough film to truly do the landscape justice, so the next day, Chaffin dug out the Jeep, drove to Green River, and wired for more film. The exploring party stayed nearly a week in Goblin Valley, camping at a site just west of today's developed campground, riding borrowed horses while exploring and photographing the hoodoos.

"Their only complaint, according to Jackson, was the lack of water (they were forced to travel ten miles to the nearest well) and the almost-constant winds blowing sand into their food," Scholl wrote.

The group broke camp on September 26, and on October 16, Arthur and his wife, Della, accompanied Tompkins to Salt Lake

City, where they described what they had seen at an informal press conference they scheduled with the *Deseret News* and *Salt Lake Tribune.*

In early 1950, the *Deseret News Magazine* published the first descriptions of Goblin Valley, and soon after, stories appeared in other Utah newspapers. Some of those journalists—like dime novel writers of the Old West—wrote the articles without even seeing the landscape for themselves.

After Tompkins began hearing about adventurous tourists seeking out the beloved geologic masterpiece he had just explored, he organized a letter-writing campaign to Congress, the Department of the Interior, and the state of Utah seeking some sort of protection for the scenic wonderland. His ultimate goal was to see the area achieve national park status.

While the National Park Service was not receptive to the idea, Utah state officials were, and in 1954, the state paid $5,600 for 2,240 acres in the valley, eventually designating it a state park in 1964. The state leased some adjoining lands from the BLM in 1984 to increase the park's land area by another one thousand acres.

If a previous name would have stuck, Goblin Valley could have become known as the "Valley of the Mushrooms"

Fun Historic Stops in Southern Utah

Goblin Valley's Geology

Upon seeing the surreal spectacle of wondrous sandstone, the inevitable question for most visitors is, "How did these get here?" The answer to that question is in an explanation of the geologic forces that formed the little "sprites."

It seems unbelievable based on what Goblin Valley visitors see today, but the park's varied goblin formations in their infancy were sediments left from an ancient sea approximately one hundred forty-five to one hundred seventy million years ago. The deeply-buried layers of sand, silt, and clay transformed into rock. Tremendous tectonic forces uplifted the area and prompted erosion that exposed those layers and began the process that fractured them, and water, wind, and frost carved them over the eons of time into what they are now.

There are four geologic layers, or "formations" as they are known, in Goblin Valley. The oldest, lowest, and most exposed layer is the Entrada sandstone, the layer where the hoodoos have formed and the same sandstone that forms the picturesque arches, fins, and spires of Arches and Capitol Reef national parks. The layers above it include the Curtis formation, then the Summerville formation, and the Morrison formation on top.

These formations form the layers of a geologic "cake," which are easily present upon closer examination, especially on the cliffs behind the main valley of goblins that exposes softer, lighter-colored layers in between harder, darker-colored layers.

In Goblin Valley, the fractured Entrada sandstone formed zones of weakness with sharp edges and corners, which are susceptible to weathering more quickly in forming the spherical-shaped goblins. The interbedded and underlying shale and siltstone, which are less resistant to weathering than the sandstone beds that form the goblin bodies, help give the goblins their stacked appearance, elongated shapes, and flat bottoms—essentially providing them a pedestal on a thin veneer of softer soil called colluvium.

Erosive forces continue to shape Goblin Valley today with older goblins toppling and weathering into oblivion. Fortunately, the process exposes new goblins.

Another Planet? Goblin Valley as a Film Location

Probably the most famous movie that utilized Goblin Valley as a filming location was *Galaxy Quest*, the 1999 film about a set of washed-up actors who once starred in a science fiction TV show much like *Star Trek* who make their money by dressing up in their costumes and attending fan conventions. A troubled alien race sees reruns of their show, thinks they're the real deal, and enlists them to help save their planet, an adventure that takes them to the planet Epsilon Gorniar II (Goblin Valley).

Former Assistant Park Manager Nathan Martinez said filming the scenes from *Galaxy Quest* in the park was a big deal but thankfully low impact.

"Nothing was allowed to be wheeled down into the valley, so it was all helicoptered into the valley and then set up," Martinez said. "They used a lot of tennis balls to mark the CGI stuff, and they also filmed some of it outside of the park on BLM property."

The park still has one of the foam hoodoos that movie crews made for filming, Martinez said, but it is not on display and lies in one of the park's sheds.

Another film that showcases the park's otherworldly scenery is the 1991 cult classic *Rubin and Ed*, in which the lead character, Rubin (played by Crispin Glover, aka George McFly in *Back to the Future*), enlists the help of luckless salesman, Ed (played by Howard Hesseman), in a quest to bury Rubin's dead cat, which is frozen in a cooler, in the Utah desert.

Parts of *City Slickers 2* and most recently, scenes of the 2011 coming-of-age drama *The Tree of Life*, starring Brad Pitt and Sean Penn, were also filmed in the park.

The "Goblin Topplers:" A Cry to Protect Resources

Goblin Valley's most recent notoriety came for a negative reason, unfortunately.

In October 2013, Boy Scout leaders Dave Hall and Glenn Taylor caused a sensation when they toppled one of the park's formations claiming that it was a safety hazard.

After discovering a rock, they thought looked loose and could fall at any moment, the duo decided that the rock posed a danger

Looking south from Goblin Valley provides a great view of the blue-looking Henry Mountains, a stark contrast to the red hues of the park's "goblins"

to hikers meandering along the trail below and took matters into their own hands. Using brute force, Taylor dislodged the massive stone and let it tumble while Hall videotaped the occasion on his phone. After it fell, Glenn Taylor and his son, Dylan, cheered and gave each other high-fives.

"Some little kid was about ready to walk down here and die, and Glenn saved his life by getting the boulder out of the way," Hall is heard saying in the video. "So it's all about saving lives here in Goblin Valley."

What ultimately got the duo in trouble was posting the video to YouTube, where it's received over five million views.

After the incident, state officials said that Hall and Taylor could be charged with anything ranging from a misdemeanor to a second-degree felony. Besides the criminal investigation, in the aftermath of the incident, Boy Scouts of America barred the two gentlemen from its organization for life, and they also received over one hundred death threats.

In a later interview with the *Salt Lake Tribune*, Hall said he realized after the incident that "state and national parks are very, very sacred to a lot of people" and that he and his friend should not have decided the fate of the goblin themselves but should have consulted park management. The state did prosecute them. They pled guilty to criminal mischief, were sentenced to probation and ordered to pay hefty fines.

The incident gave the park attention, but not in the way park managers desired.

"We received numerous phone calls from around the world," Martinez said. "I think it was also a bit of a new precedent in that our county wasn't exactly sure about how to prosecute it."

One Utah lawmaker even proposed a bill specifically banning goblin toppling, but it never became law.

In the wake of the topplers' episode, Goblin Valley's visitation steadily increased, which prompted park management to make a renewed effort to help educate visitors on preserving the park's resources by treading lightly. In addition to keeping up with the influx of visitors and educating them about protecting resources, one of the park's main challenges is exacerbated by its remoteness: maintenance.

"It's not like we can just run over to the hardware store to fix a facilities problem," Martinez said. "We try to keep a lot of maintenance supplies on hand—and we have a fantastic region crew that provides a lot of support for big issues—but we are still working hard on keeping our solar and well systems up to date with the increased visitation."

When asked about current visitation numbers in contrast to the park's early days, Martinez said, "We are close to two hundred thousand visitors a year these days. So yes, I would say we are on the map now."

Visiting Goblin Valley

Goblin Valley is like a giant playground for children, who will enjoy climbing on the goblins (most of which are not very high off the ground) of various shapes and sizes. Photo opportunities abound as each hoodoo is different from the last. The park features a visitor center, a large covered pavilion overlooking the main Valley of the Goblins, three established hiking trails, and a campground.

Interpretive programs are also available, including ranger-guided moonlight hikes and night sky tours, which offer prime stargazing opportunities because of the park's dark night sky.

Goblin Valley can be a springboard to visit other nearby scenic places such as Little Wildhorse Canyon and Bell Canyon, located in the San Rafael Swell and managed by the Bureau of Land Management.

The best times to visit are spring and fall when the temperatures are milder.

The original story and photo gallery can be found at the following link:

https://www.stgeorgeutah.com/news/archive/2018/04/08/goblin-valley-day-a-late-explored-otherworldly-erosive-spectacle/

FOR FURTHER INFORMATION
Goblin Valley State Park website:

https://stateparks.utah.gov/parks/goblin-valley/

*The Parry Lodge, still in operation today, was
ground zero for western moviemaking in
Kanab during its heyday in the 1940s, 1950s, and 1960s*

8

KANAB WESTERN MOVIEMAKING
Hollywood's Former Number One Branch Location

In the 1940s, it became known as "Utah's Hollywood" because of its rising stock as a filming location for films of the Western genre, which was the most popular sort of film at the time. Most said the sweeping landscapes looked fantastic in Technicolor.

However, in the 1930s, Kanab was the town in the U.S. farthest away from a railroad for its size and had a population of fewer than thirteen hundred residents—not a place that seemed destined for movie setting stardom.

Kanab's fame as a place most Americans would see on the silver screen or on TV in their living room can largely be attributed to a set of three brothers, the Parrys, who gave movie studios the whole package—a full-service arrangement that included location scouting, lodging, transportation, catering, and livestock, as well as carriages and covered wagons, James D'Arc wrote in his book, *When Hollywood Came to Town: A History of Moviemaking in Utah*. It wasn't just the Parry brothers—Chauncey, Whit, and Gronway—doing all the work, though. Nearly the entire town chipped in, serving as extras, wranglers, drivers, and laborers. Townspeople even hosted movie stars and crew members when the town's few motels had no vacancies.

The Parry Lodge essentially became the headquarters for major studios filming in the area. The Lodge started as a small, three-bedroom house owned by Justin Johnson. Chauncey Parry purchased the home in 1928, then a parcel of land directly north of the home in 1938, on which he built additional rooms, D'Arc wrote. He started expanding the home in March 1931, constructing what he called "summer cabins" just north and west of the central building and opened for its first tourist season in June 1931, at which time only two movies had been filmed in the Kanab area, *Deadwood Coach* and *The Big Trail*.

Business wasn't brisk at first, but Chauncey Parry made frequent trips to Hollywood with pictures of Kanab and the surrounding area in hand to meet with location scouts and studio executives to convince them to make their movies in Southern Utah. By 1938, the Parry brothers had started "to perfect their integrated system of negotiating with studios for locations (Chauncey), transportation and vintage wagons (Gronway), and food and lodging (Whit)," D'Arc explained.

A colorful local rancher, Merle "Cowhide" Adams, began working closely with the Parrys in the 1930s, handling the wrangling of livestock and horses for films, starting with *The Dude Ranger* in 1934 and continuing into the early 1970s.

"Cowhide's infectious personality also got him on-screen parts in a number of films, some of them with dialogue," D'Arc remarked. "Whether teaching young Roddy McDowall how to rope for the 'Flicka' pictures or working with Fred MacMurray on *Smoky*, Cowhide Adams was a favorite of Hollywood movie crews and executives alike."

Another local who was good with stock served as an extra in numerous films over the years and made many of the arrangements with the studios was Fay Hamblin, a grandson of early pioneer leader Jacob Hamblin.

The Parrys even invested some of their own money in the first movie filmed completely in the Kanab area, *Feud on the Range*, in 1939, which was followed by three other low-budget movies, one of which, *The Mormon Conquest*, was based on the settlement of Kane County. It had a short life, however, as its premiere in Kanab on July 11 and 12, 1939, appears to be the only showings of the film, and all copies of it have been lost.

Also, in the late 1930s, a group of fourteen prominent Kanab residents became investors in the newly incorporated Security National Pictures, which constructed a forty by sixty-foot covered stage with an adjacent Western street in 1939, D'Arc noted. They called it "Utah's Hollywood," which was added to the masthead of the *Kane County Standard* newspaper beginning with the September 1, 1939, issue. The first major studio to do a movie in Kanab was MGM, who filmed *The Bad Man of Brimstone* there in 1938 and followed that up a few years later with *Billy the Kid*.

One movie filmed in the area with a lot of fanfare—a huge premiere in Salt Lake City with the stars of the show speaking to sold-out theaters—was *Brigham Young* in 1940 with Dean Jagger in the title role. Even Heber J. Grant, president of The Church of Jesus Christ of Latter-day Saints at the time, called the movie a "friend maker," D'Arc wrote.

Several other big movies were filmed in the area soon after, including *Western Union*, based on Zane Grey's final novel, *Can't Stop Singing*, a Western musical, and *Arabian Nights*, in which the area served as a stand-in for the Middle East, with the Coral Pink Sand Dunes as one of the stars of the show. Production of the movie required the construction of a road to the dunes, which was fully supported by the state of Utah's newly formed Department of Publicity and Industrial Development.

The two staple backdrops for filming in the area, where numerous set-pieces went up and down over the years, were Angel (or Kanab) Canyon, also known as Kanab Movie Ranch (north of town and now home to Best Friends Animal Sanctuary) and Johnson Canyon, located northeast of town.

A 1945 *Saturday Evening Post* article titled "The Town that Learned to Act" by Florabel Muir called Kanab "Hollywood's main factory branch."

"It's facilities, elaborate and constantly expanding, are available to all studios," Muir touted in her article. "The region has more than fifteen hundred experienced film players on-call, including the neighboring Paiute and Navajo Indians."

Some Kanabites even "donned a breechcloth and brown make-up" to play attacking Indians in some of the movies shot in the area, D'Arc wrote. According to Muir, Kanab's actors had the advantage of not having to pay Screen Actors Guild dues, since the guild's authority did not reach farther than three hundred miles from Hollywood.

Muir said that Kanab's adult population was one hundred percent movie actors, albeit actors who had never seen the actual Hollywood and never cared if they did.

"Everybody else in the world, it seems, wants to take a gander at the film lots and the stars," Muir wrote. "Kanab can take 'em or leave 'em, and it does both with the utmost nonchalance."

The author's daughters and a friend take in the view of Kanab Canyon, known today as Angel Canyon, which was a filming site of western movies during Kanab's moviemaking heyday

And by the same token, Muir noted, seeing big Hollywood stars didn't excite Kanab residents of the time, either.

"A flock of screen stars strolling down Kanab's dusty main street excites no more curiosity than a stray sheepdog chasing its tail," she wrote.

In addition to her commentary on Kanab's populace of the time, Muir gushed over how its nearby scenery appeared on film.

"The color camera translates to the screen paintings of breathtaking loveliness," she wrote. "If you're a movie fan, you've visited this grandiose fairyland by proxy many times."

Despite all the superlatives of its surrounding red rock spectacle, however, there were several cases in which movie crews painted Southern Utah's red sandstone so the colors would show up better on camera.

Muir, like D'Arc, was clear, however, that Kanab's fame as a moviemaking mecca did not come by chance, but by the hard work of the Parry brothers, who with their package deals gave any studio filming in Kanab a major bang for their buck. According to Muir, once a film company arrived in Kanab, their worries were virtually over.

The Parrys would provide accommodations and food service at Parry Lodge, as well as transportation for the actors, cameras, technicians, and "all the impedimenta of a movie troupe," Muir noted.

Kanab even had its own casting office, housed in an old gas station, where any type of actor, "from an Indian chief to a bathing beauty," could be provided at a moment's notice, she wrote. For their efforts in facilitating moviemaking, the Parry Brothers made approximately $30,000 in 1944, according to Muir's story, which doesn't sound like much, but would be over $400,000 in today's dollars.

Into the 1950s and 1960s, Kanab remained a staple for Western moviemaking, including hits such as *Buffalo Bill* starring Joel McCrea; *Pony Express* starring Charlton Heston; and *Sergeants 3* starring "Rat Pack" members Frank Sinatra, Dean Martin, and Sammy Davis Jr.

In the 1950s, Westerns were as popular as ever.

"For most of the 1950s, Westerns accounted for between eighteen to thirty-four percent of feature films, and, by the end of the decade, there were forty-eight Western series showing up each week on television," D'Arc wrote.

During these two decades, several Western TV series were filmed in the Kanab area, including *Death Valley Days*, *Have Gun-Will Travel*, *Daniel Boone*, *How the West Was Won* and, most notably, *Gunsmoke*, whose home base was the Johnson Canyon set.

However, all movies filmed in the Kanab area were not Westerns. One grand departure was *The Girl in Black Stockings*, a movie whose plot was much like Alfred Hitchcock's *Psycho*, but predated it. The film was primarily shot at Parry Lodge itself and a few other locations around Kanab. Another was *The Greatest Story Ever Told*, chronicling the life of Jesus Christ and filmed largely in Glen Canyon before it was inundated by Lake Powell.

By the last half of the 1970s, however, the Western genre was on its way out, which signaled the end of major moviemaking in Kanab. The last major Western films shot in the area were *The Outlaw Josey Wales*, which starred Clint Eastwood, in 1976, and Walt Disney's Western spoof, *The Apple Dumpling Gang Rides Again*, in 1978, starring comedians Don Knotts and Tim Conway.

D'Arc wrote that the filming of Disney's satirical Western proved a symbol of the demise of the Western and Kanab's place as a significant filming location for the genre, as a movie fort built in 1953 was severely damaged during production and never repaired.

"More than a half-century of moviemaking and movie promoting had come to an end," D'Arc explained. "In its stead remains the old movie town in Johnson Canyon: a weathered, crumbling ghost, a fading witness to a time when Buffalo Bill Cody, Kit Carson, Wild Bill Hickok, the Lone Ranger, the Western Union company, George Custer, Matt Dillon, Paladin, Daniel Boone, Black Bart, Calamity Jane, Smoky, our 'friend' Flicka—and a camel or two—occupied the same expanse of real estate."

Many businesses in Kanab key on its reputation as a prime location to film Western movies such as this display featuring a figure resembling John Wayne at Denny's Wigwam

Visiting Kanab: The Legacy Today

Even though Kanab's golden age of moviemaking is over (there have been parts of a few films shot in the area since the late 1970s), the legacy of that golden age lives on. Parry Lodge is still going strong and boasts a large gallery of portraits of movie stars who once stayed there during its heyday.

Businesses on Kanab's main drag sell many different wares as remembrances of its former glory, and one in particular, Denny's Wigwam, plays up the Western-film backlot motif with everything from a horse-drawn carriage ideal for a photo opp to wisecracks emanating from a mannequin in an outhouse.

The Little Hollywood Museum boasts set pieces actually used in *The Outlaw Josey Wales*, which were formerly located in Angel Canyon near Best Friends Animal Sanctuary. Made to look like adobe, the set pieces are actually made of fiberglass. The museum offers visitors the chance to don Western props for pictures with an honest-to-goodness Western movie backdrop.

Fun Historic Stops in Southern Utah

The museum also includes a restaurant serving chuckwagon meals, a photography studio, and a gift shop.

Some of the sets in Johnson Canyon are still standing but are on private land and very dilapidated after years of neglect.

In addition to the physical reminders of the Western moviemaking legacy is the annual Western Legends Heritage and Music Festival Kanab hosts every August that features a variety of events with actors who once starred in Western films as well as a parade with longhorn cattle, a wagon train, historic movie bus tours and a barbecue contest, among others.

The original story and photo gallery can be found at the following link:

https://www.stgeorgeutah.com/news/archive/2019/04/21/raw-kanab-western-moviemaking-day-its-stint-as-the-no-1-hollywood-branch-location/

FOR FURTHER INFORMATION
Little Hollywood Museum website:

http://www.littlehollywoodmuseum.org

Kodachrome Basin is a red sandstone showcase featuring numerous sand pipe formations that look like narrow columns

9

KODACHROME BASIN STATE PARK
A 'Blank Spot' on the Map to a Photographer's Paradise, Southern Utah Base Camp

Chimney Rock would have been such a mundane name for what many see as a magical place. There are so many "chimney rocks" in other places, including one in Colorado that became a national monument in 2012.

However, Kodachrome Basin, a wonderland of stone spires just over twenty-two miles from Bryce Canyon National Park (and able to be seen from that park's Inspiration Point), became a state park in 1962. This name was chosen because a moniker placed on it just over a decade earlier was copyrighted.

Thankfully, later on, Kodak granted its permission for the Kodachrome name to stick, and the only park in the nation named after a brand of film became a reality.

In fact, Kodak helped pay for early park brochures, and each one had an advertisement for Kodak on the back page.

Geologic History

Some geologists have surmised that the park's unique landscape once resembled Yellowstone National Park, believing the sand pipes are remnants of solidified sediment that filled ancient geysers.

Believe it or not, according to geologists, Kodachrome Basin State Park is one hundred eighty million years old. Located on the Colorado Plateau, an uplifted region that covers the four corners area of Utah, Arizona, Colorado and New Mexico. The park's exposed rock formations range from the Jurassic Period (one hundred eighty million years ago) to the Cretaceous Period (ninety-five million years ago). The park showcases a rock layer from each of these periods, telling the story of an inland sea that once covered this now desert landscape and testifying to the relentless erosive forces of wind and water.

The oldest of these layers, the Carmel Formation reveals solid layers of the mineral gypsum, "which forms white striations in the red-colored cliffs in the lower elevations of the park," the park's current map and guide say.

The red-hued Entrada Formation, which lies just above the Carmel Formation, is a solidified composition of fine-grained sandstone as well as clay, gypsum, quartz, and clay.

"This formation is one of the most scenic in the park due to its color," the map and guide explained. "It also forms the ubiquitous 'slickrock' of Southern Utah. Most of the sedimentary pipes found within the park occur in this formation."

Just above the Entrada is the Henrieville Sandstone layer, which was deposited near the end of the Jurassic Period. This layer exhibits a white to tan appearance and is almost unnoticedable in the main part of the park, but Grosvenor Arch, located eleven miles south of the park within the boundaries of Grand Staircase Escalante National Monument, showcases this layer.

The Dakota and Tropic Shale formations make up the top layer, deposited approximately ninety-five million years ago when "a vast seaway covered much of the interior of North America, including most of Utah," the map and guide states.

The main attraction at the park is its array of sixty-seven sedimentary pipes jutting up from the valley floor ranging in height from six to one hundred seventy feet, which is the height of Chimney Rock. Geologists are unsure exactly how these stately spires formed but have a few theories. One theory is that earthquakes caused coarse, water-saturated sediment to scour pathways that eventually filled up again and were recemented with a harder rock that remained while constant erosion removed the layers surrounding it. Another theory is the pipes are the remnants of ancient springs, which became choked with sediments that became more erosive resistant than the surrounding rock.

A more recent theory suggests that the pipes formed from water-saturated pockets buried under layers of other sediments over millions of years.

"Pressure from the overlying sediments forced the wet slurry upwards," the map and guide explained. "The rising slurry scoured pathways through the overlying rock, eventually cementing into hard rock. Erosion stripped away the softer rock layers revealing the landscape you see today."

The National Geographic Society Expedition

Before 1948, cattlemen and their herds were really the only ones aware of what would become the state park. In fact, Aaron Farmer, who served as the park manager from 2005 to 2014 before taking over as park manager at Green River State Park, described an old cattle trail along the backside of the park that led to nearby Henrieville. The trail is extremely steep and narrow but cut off thirty-five miles and a couple days' travel.

Farmer said he has heard tales from old-timers saying that once in a while, some cows and donkeys would lose their footing on the trail and fall to their deaths or severely injure themselves. Another story he recounted is that, without fences in the area, sometimes the early cattlemen would string ropes together and tie blankets on them to keep the cattle contained.

Today's Kodachrome Basin visitors can see why it deserves its name with its vast array of colorful rock formations of different shapes and sizes

Until the mid-20th century, Kodachrome Basin was "a blank spot on the map," Farmer said.

Photographers from the National Geographic Society hoped to change that fact and came to the area on a photography expedition in 1948. They nicknamed the area "Kodachrome Flat" after Kodak's famous film, known for its rich color saturation, and for its wide use by National Geographic photographers during the first decades it printed its magazines in color. It is no surprise these mid-20th-century photographers felt the way they did after seeing it due to the multi-colored spires' stark contrast with brilliant blue skies.

The expedition, headed by writer/photographer Jack Breed, included fifteen people, three jeeps, two trucks, and thirty-five horses. Breed wrote the article that chronicled the expedition published in the September 1949 issue of the magazine entitled "First Motor Sortie into Escalante Land."

In his June 2009 article (which includes some of the original pictures that appeared in the 1949 article) lamenting the discontinuation of Kodachrome Film, *National Geographic Traveler*

Senior Photo Editor Dan Westergren said the expedition "was hoping to find unknown and yet unnamed geographical oddities in the hidden cliffs and canyons."

As recorded in his article, this was Breed's first assessment of the area:

> "It was a beautiful and fantastic country. A mile to the left near the base of the cliff, I could see red pinnacles thrust up from the valley floor. The few natives who had been here called this area 'Thorny Pasture,' but we renamed it 'Kodachrome Flat' because of the astonishing variety of contrasting colors in the formations. Huge rocks, towers, pinnacles, fins, and fans surrounded us. Everywhere the results of erosion could be seen in all stages."

Breed admitted that, despite its beauty, exploring the "wild and forbidding" area was tough because "heat, sand and sudden storms test men and cars" but still called the area they named "a photographer's dream come true."

During their trip, Breed and his crew did discover an arch, as they were hoping, and they named it after the president of the National Geographic Society at the time, Dr. Gilbert Grosvenor. Westergren joked that Breed might have done this to ensure his job security, but as Breed described it, it was because he was "the man who, we all agreed, had done more than any other person to arouse public interest in geography."

The aspect of the arch that most impressed Breed was its color, which, as explained earlier, is its location in a different rock layer—Navajo sandstone instead of the Entrada sandstone most common in the park.

"This striking natural bridge is carved from creamy rock, a rarity in a land of brilliant reds," Breed explained. "Actually, it is a double arch, with the larger span on the end of a buttress that juts from the main sandstone butte."

The arch is one hundred fifty feet above the ground and ninety-two feet wide. The arch is not part of Kodachrome Basin, however. It is actually within the boundaries of Grand Staircase-Escalante

National Monument but has always been closely associated with the park.

Kodachrome Basin became a state park mainly due to the big push from the Bryce Valley Lions Club, Farmer said, which features members from the surrounding towns of Tropic, Cannonville, and Henrieville, all of which lie in Garfield County. The park, nine miles south of Cannonville, is actually in Kane County but is obviously more tied to Garfield County, he explained.

Today the park is surrounded on three sides by Grand Staircase-Escalante National Monument, an entity that did not exist when it was designated in the early 1960s.

What's in a Name?

Kodachrome Basin State Park is full of unofficial place names. In the park, a visitor will find many rock formations that have sparked the imagination of visitors old and new, including Sherlock Holmes Spire, Fred Flintstone, The Hamburger, and The White Buffalo. Most names in the park stem from old-timers who have run cattle in or near the park, the late Tom Shakespeare, a long-time park manager and Tropic local said in an interview with the author in 2000.

One of the monuments in the park that may be the most controversial is known as "Big Stoney." Other names in use for the gray sandstone cylinder standing about fifteen to twenty feet high, which greets visitors near the entrance of the park, include "Fair Maiden's Dream" and "Paul Bunyan's Boot," Shakespeare said, who noted that the landform is clearly a phallic symbol.

Campground site No. 17 near the base of the spire is often termed the "Honeymoon Suite," Farmer noted.

One official name the park does possess is Ballerina Spire, which clearly looks like a ballerina's leg, Shakespeare said. Other official fanciful include Angel's Palace, Big Bear Geyser, and The Hat Shop.

Even before it was called Chimney Rock, the park was formerly known as Thorley's Pasture (after rancher Tom Thorley, who used it for grazing his cattle), or as Breed pointed out, Thorny Pasture (after the abundant cacti).

*Most of Kodachrome Basin's formations are easily
viewable from the road or short hiking trails*

Shakespeare left his own mark on the park. An arch in the park was named after him. Shakespeare told the story of discovering it while looking for a coyote den in 1976. He said he checked around to see if anyone knew about it, but apparently, no one did.

Farmer, however, said that local ranchers knew about it.

Even in his article in 1949, Breed writes of asking local rancher John Johnson about the existence of arches or natural bridges in the area.

"Yes, I've heard tell of one or two, but in my forty years here, I've never seen any," the rancher reported. "I'm always too busy looking for stray cattle or good grass feed to notice the scenery."

A local contest named the arch, choosing to recognize not only Shakespeare but also his father, over alternatives such as "Tom Thumb's Arch." Unfortunately, that arch collapsed in April 2019, a testament to the continuing force of erosion. Visitors can still hike the six hundred-yard trail to see where the arch was. There are other scenic attractions along the trail still worth viewing.

"Sentinel Spire is still on the Shakespeare Trail and is worth going out to visit, and the Slickrock cutoff has some of the best views in the park and is a great trail for photography," said current Park Manager Nathan Martinez.

Kodachrome Basin Today

In the past, Kodachrome Basin was a place for those seeking a little solitude away from the crowds of nearby Bryce Canyon. Since 2010, visitor numbers have increased significantly, and the campground, especially in the warmer months, is usually full. Still, many campers use it as a base camp to explore nearby attractions as far away as Zion, Farmer said.

Kodachrome Basin is better known to Europeans than visitors in the United States, Farmer explained. One story he recounted proving this was a set of milk bottle stickers produced in the Netherlands showcasing U.S. national parks. Even though it is not a national park, Kodachrome Basin was included in that series of stickers.

"A lot of our visitors are on the Grand Circle tour—working their way from the Grand Canyon up to Zion, then to Bryce, Capitol Reef, and finally to Arches and Canyonlands," Martinez said. "This trip seems to be advertised pretty heavily among Europeans. The majority of our foreign visitors are German, with a few from France, the Netherlands, and Britain. They usually come in the summer because they don't know that it's our hot season, and most of the locals are up in the mountains rather than down in the desert."

During the campground's peak season, Farmer said people speaking English in the campground are in the minority. The language campers hear the most, it seems, is German, as it seems German tourists are the ones who keep coming back year after year.

In Farmer's opinion, the Kodachrome Basin campground is one of the best state park campgrounds in Utah because it is well laid out and recently added seven hookup sites as well as eighteen additional campsites in two different loops, called Arch and Bryce View.

"We also added two cabins to the park which offer more of a glamping experience," Martinez said. "They have bunk beds and a futon provided and sleep up to six people. We are also well known for having some of the best bathrooms of any campgrounds. Our maintenance guy Brandon (Baugh), has done an incredible job of tiling the bathrooms and installing rainfall showers in the basin and oasis bathrooms."

Visiting Kodachrome Basin

Kodachrome Basin features several hiking, biking, and equestrian trails throughout the park of varying difficulty levels. The Grand Parade, Shakespeare Arch, and Angel's Palace trails are some of the easier ones while Eagle's View Overlook is one of its more challenging.

Spring and fall are particularly pleasant seasons to visit the park as it does not feel too hot.

The original story and photo gallery can be found at the following link:

https://www.stgeorgeutah.com/news/ archive/2019/11/03/kodachrome-basin-day- a-blank-spot-on-the-map-to-a- photographers-paradise-southern-utah- base-camp

FOR FURTHER INFORMATION
Goblin Valley State Park website:

https://stateparks.utah.gov/parks/koda chrome-basin/

By sheer luck, the kiln built by Old Irontown's original settlers to make charcoal survives today

10

OLD IRONTOWN
'Utah's First Ghost Town' Provides a Peek Into Pioneer Iron Production

There is a good reason Iron County bears that name.

When the area was first settled in 1851, Brigham Young, the second president of The Church of Jesus Christ of Latter-day Saints, had visions of a self-sufficient society and wanted to take advantage of the iron deposits discovered in the area to produce much-needed iron products. To try to complete that vision, Young called families to Southern Utah to work in the church's "Iron Mission."

Despite brimming optimism, the church's first try at iron production right after the first settlers arrived in Cedar City didn't go very well. By 1858, it closed, not having produced iron of the quality needed to help the pioneer effort.

"Such fruitless exertions to make iron seems to be exhausting not only the patience, but the vital energies, and power of the settlement," Young wrote in an October 8, 1858 letter signaling the close of what was called the Deseret Iron Company.

Ten years later a group of settlers was ready to try it again, but this time it wasn't a church-run enterprise, it was basically a venture capital operation envisioned by wealthy merchant Ebenezer Hanks, said Ryan Paul, former Frontier Homestead State Park Museum curator and current Southern Utah University history professor. This time its location was approximately twenty-four miles south-west of Cedar City on the banks of Pinto Creek. Fittingly, it was christened "Iron City."

Peter Shirts discovered the site, and others deemed it an excellent place for a city that could support five thousand residents with adequate water, coal, building rock, and clay for bricks.

Hanks organized the Union Iron Company (later the Great Western Iron Company) in June 1868 and served as its president with Shirts, said to be a quiet, restless man, serving as one of the directors, perhaps as a reward for discovering the location's iron deposits. Some of the iron laborers who populated the town had been part of the first attempt to manufacture iron.

Exempt from territorial taxes, at first, the town grew rapidly. The 1870 census noted that there were nineteen households and a total of ninety-seven residents living in Iron City. In 1875, there were a few hundred residents. By 1871 the town boasted a brick schoolhouse, boarding house, general store, butcher shop, and even a post office. That same year, its furnace with a capacity of twenty-five hundred pounds became operational. A major reorganization of the company in 1873 resulted in the construction of a new blast furnace, air furnace, pattern shop, and company office.

The company also had two kilns used to smolder juniper and pinyon wood in an oxygen-reduced environment to produce the charcoal used to process the iron. It took approximately twelve days for one kiln to produce 50 bushels of charcoal, which was enough fuel to produce one ton of iron, according to an interpretive sign near the lone existing kiln.

Much like Silver Reef to the south, many of the workers who

came to work in the iron industry were not Latter-day Saints, giving the town a more raucous reputation as a center for drinking and swearing. In addition to laborers, some non-Mormon consultants were brought in to advise the operation. Some of these non-Mormons were intent on breaking theocratic economic power, but Iron City directors were firmly intent on keeping the venture conformed to Latter-day Saint economic ideals, according to Kerry Bate in an article, "Iron City, Mormon Mining Town," which appeared in the winter 1982 issue of the *Utah Historical Quarterly*.

During its short lifetime, Iron City supplied ore to the Utah Western Railroad, some Nevada mining companies, and, most notably, the iron used to sculpt the twelve oxen that support the St. George Temple's baptismal font. The bulk of what the company manufactured, however, were small items such as andirons (bracket supports where logs were laid for fireplaces), hand irons for ironing clothes as well as bootjacks made in the shape of pine beetles, among others. Selling these small items to poverty-stricken settlers was no way to raise adequate capital.

The problem facing Iron City was logistics, Paul said, because it was difficult to transport the iron to outside markets, and the company could only sell the products it made to the local popularition for so long. In fact, one of the original company's founders, Seth Blair wrote to the *Deseret News*, pleading the erection of a foundry somewhere in Utah that could turn the company's cast iron into steel or wrought iron, but to no avail.

Ironically, the town grew rapidly just before its demise. For example, the monthly payroll between 1874 and 1875 rose from $500 to $4,000, Bate reported. At its peak, Iron City's furnace produced eight hundred pounds of quality iron about every eight hours.

Transportation challenges were one of the big reasons Iron City's manufacturing did not take off. For example, in 1874, it cost $40 per ton to freight iron from Iron City to Salt Lake City. Railroad competition was lowering freight rates from the east, making eastern iron cheaper.

Plans were in place to build a railroad spur from Salt Lake City to Iron City with a route that would travel through other mining districts, thinking the demand for iron in Salt Lake City would justify it. Hanks also dreamed of building a narrow-gauge railroad to the Colorado River to tap into southern markets. None of these ambitious transportation plans ever materialized, however.

The panic of 1874, an economic downturn, contributed to the company's failure as did competition from several other iron companies in the territory, including the Ogden Iron Works, the Utah Central Iron Company, and the City Creek Iron Mine.

Another problem that signaled the death knell of iron production was the lack of sufficient local capital to keep the business going and to possibly expand it. Despite many attempts to attract outside investors, Hanks and his company's attempts fell short. Additionally, in 1874, when the board of directors nearly had some much-needed cash in hand to keep the ironworks going, they wrote Young for advice on the situation, and he advised against taking the capital, preaching the United Order at the time.

"The board as a whole felt that the purpose of the iron industry was to build up the kingdom, not to build up the iron industry at the cost of the kingdom," Bate wrote.

Iron production ceased in 1876, but residents remained in the company town into the 1880s, giving it the distinction of "Utah's first ghost town."

The LDS church actually tried to revive iron production in the 1880s and even started grading a railroad line between the coal mines near Cedar City, the iron deposits at Iron Mountain and Iron City's furnaces, but church leaders were forced into hiding to avoid prosecution for polygamy and were unable to pursue development of the new company.

The dreams of these pioneer industrialists to exploit the county's vast iron deposits were not realized until after 1923, the year the railroad finally came to Iron County. With the railroad in place, Columbia Steel Works began production in 1924. U.S. Steel purchased Columbia in 1935 and soon after shifted its operations to Iron Mountain, expending millions of dollars that successfully harnessed the underground wealth through open-pit blasting. For a time, iron mining was a major economic engine of the county. Iron mining, however, ceased in the mid-1980s largely due to soaring production costs and price undercutting by foreign sources.

Evidence of this golden age of iron mining can be seen on the mountainsides near Old Irontown.

An old chimney is one of the remnants visitors see while strolling along the trail in Old Irontown, considered Utah's first ghost town

Old Irontown Today

Truthfully, detailed information about Iron City, which morphed into the name Old Irontown, is not available.

"We don't know much about it," Paul said. "There are no plat maps. We're still figuring out how they built the furnaces and where the water came from. It's an archaeological puzzle."

With no plat map, there is no way of knowing the location of buildings whose ruins did not withstand the test of time. Even information about buildings whose ruins are still visible is lacking. For example, no one knows who lived in the home whose ruins still stand east of the kiln along the park's trail.

Paul said the one intact kiln is there by sheer luck because, over the years, locals have taken many stones from the ruins to use in their own homes, especially in their fireplaces.

The Sons of Utah Pioneers group has played a large role in ensuring the stabilization of the kiln. For example, approximately every ten years, the mortar is repointed, which involves removing loose mortar joints and refilling them.

Archaeological work has gone on there in the past, Paul said, but it's expensive.

Measures taken to try to prevent looting and destruction are controlling access to the ruins with a fence surrounding it, Paul said, as well as installing a railing inside the intact kiln so visitors can only go so far into it.

Old Irontown is surrounded by many private residences. Paul said the infrastructure is out there because the area was going to be an MX Missile site in the 1980s, but those plans never materialized.

The ghost town was in private hands until 2000 when the landowners donated it to the state, at which time it became an unstaffed satellite state park operated by Frontier Homestead State Park (formerly known as Iron Mission State Park) in Cedar City. At the time of this writing, it is slated to become a state monument.

Paul said only about five to six thousand visitors see Old Irontown each year, but that visitation is hard to track because the best record they have is the visitor log at the site.

Some locals have even admitted to Paul that they've driven that stretch of Highway 56, he said, and have never taken the time to stop and see it.

"Most people who go out there really enjoy it," Paul said.

Fun Historic Stops in Southern Utah

Visiting Old Irontown

Old Irontown is located nearly twenty-four miles southwest of Cedar City via Highway 56. Approaching it from the east, one will see the Old Irontown sign along the highway. Turn left (south) off the highway just after the sign and proceed three miles until reaching the ruins.

Once parked, take the Discovery Trail, which leads visitors past all of the existing ruins at the site, including the intact kiln and the remains of the old molding house, whose most prominent feature is its nearly intact chimney. Do not miss heading east along the trail through the juniper and pinyon pine forest to the remains of a private residence.

Interpretive signs explain a little about the site's history, and little plaques identify some of the ruins as well as some of the plant life in the area.

The ruins make an excellent picnic spot complete with a pavilion and pit toilets.

The original story and photo gallery can be found at the following link:

https://www.stgeorgeutah.com/news/archive/2018/05/06/raw-old-irontown-day-utahs-first-ghost-town-provides-a-peek-into-pioneer-iron-production/

FOR FURTHER INFORMATION
Frontier Homestead State Park Old Irontown web page:

https://frontierhomestead.org/homestead-telegraph/2016/11/10/old-iron-town

A model of what Orderville looked like when it lived by the United Order sits in the town's restored Zion's Cooperative Mercantile Institution store

11

ORDERVILLE
The Longest Attempt at Living the United Order

The saying goes that one person or group's utopia is another's dystopia, and such was the case with the settlement of Orderville, the longest-running and most successful attempt in the early history of The Church of Jesus Christ of Latter-day Saints to live the United Order.

The United Order was an attempt at a utopia—basically, divinely-appointed communism before communism as the world now knows it even existed. This notion of communal living, in which all things in a community are held in common with all provided for and "no rich or poor among them," was advocated by Brigham Young, the second president of the church. In fact, a

General Conference talk Orson Pratt gave in April 1874 admonished church members to live by this ideal as part of a way to overcome the economic depression known as the Panic of 1873. Some rejected it, others tried to live it and failed quickly, but one group had staying power—saints who named their community after the communal system they were striving to make work.

They first tried it in Mount Carmel, but there was too much dissension and resistance, so just like the Nephites of the Book of Mormon, this set of settlers who were truly committed to living the Order broke off from the group and moved two and a half miles north to found Orderville. The location proved an excellent spot to establish such a communal atmosphere because of its isolation at the time.

Settlers began arriving in Orderville in 1870 and 1871, but the United Order itself did not begin until July 14, 1875. Whatever cash and goods Order members possessed beforehand were given to the Order, so everyone would be equal. Prospective members were even asked a set of twenty questions, much like today's temple recommend interview, to see if they were truly committed. Questions ranged from "Do you use tobacco, tea or coffee?" to "Are you in the habit of quarreling?"

Homes were hastily constructed with wood framing in a square with a communal dining hall, which was next to the bishop's house, known as "The Big House" because it was literally the largest among the dwellings, in the middle. Operated like a military establishment, a bugle sounded at 7 a.m., noon, and 6 p.m. to call members to breakfast, lunch, and dinner. Curfew was at 9 p.m.

Members of the Order later remarked that one of the things that truly made them feel like a community and built camaraderie was the fact that they always ate together. At first, the adults and children sat together during meals, but later, whole families were allowed to sit together.

Each member of the order received equal pay for their work. Adult males received $1.50 per day, and boys ages eleven to seventeen received 75 cents. Apparently, the Order didn't feel women's work was equal to the men because they only received 75 cents a day as well. These wages went into a member's account, which was debited whenever that member purchased goods from the Order. But at the end of the year, if one's account was overdrawn because of illness or any other catastrophe, surpluses on other accounts made up the difference, and at the start of the new year, the playing field was equal again.

The Order strove to be self-contained, trying not to even rely on imports from neighboring towns. It had its own bakery, blacksmith shop, cabinet shop, dairy, lumber mill, shoe shop, and woolen factory as well as significant herds of sheep and cattle. Members grew and made nearly everything they needed, from soap to pants. They sold their surplus goods to neighboring towns for cash and built up a capital fund to buy equipment and land and even invested in enterprises outside the community.

In the mind of the current Second Counselor in the church's First Presidency, there was another reason the Order lasted as long as it did: the gratitude of its members, especially a faction who had suffered great privations on the banks of the Muddy River in Nevada.

"When those who had been called to the Muddy were released, they were in near destitution," President Henry B. Eyring said in a talk given at the October 1989 General Conference, then First Counselor of the Presiding Bishopric. "They didn't have much, but their poverty may have been their greatest contribution. Having almost nothing provided a basis for future comparison that might have guaranteed gratitude: any food or clothing or housing that came to them in Orderville would be treasure compared to their privation on the Muddy mission."

In fact, accounts of several members of the Order written later on, say that the time they lived the Order was one of the happiest times of their lives. For instance, former Order member Henry Fowler remembered, as reported in Martha Sonntag Bradley's *A History of Kane County*:

> *"I have lived in Utah, Arizona, California, Idaho, and in many different towns, and I never was so much attached to a people; I never experienced greater joy nor had better times than during the period of time I was connected to the United Order of Orderville."*

99

Today, the Orderville skyline looks much different than during the days of the United Order more than a century ago

But unfortunately, envy became part of the Order's undoing, leading to some members' slightly dystopian view of the organization. First of all, its isolation was eroding with the railroad and telegraph drawing closer. The fact that the economy was improving in surrounding towns augmented that envy.

"The people in Orderville were living better than they had in years, but the memory of poverty on the Muddy had faded," Eyring said. "They now focused on what was in the next town. And so they felt old-fashioned and deprived."

One story Eyring told that illustrated this envy is the tale of a boy who acted on his discontent over being denied a new pair of pants from the Orderville factory because his were not sufficiently worn out. In secret, he gathered the docked lambs' tails from the spring crop, sheared the wool, and stored it in sacks. When he was assigned to take a load of wool to sell in Nephi, he took the sacks of wool he'd obtained from the lambs' tails and exchanged it for a pair of store pants. When he returned, he was all the rage when he wore those pants to the next dance.

When the president of the Order questioned him about what he had done, the boy was honest. At a meeting called specifically to address the issue, the leaders of the Order commended him for his ingenuity but determined that the pants really belonged to the Order and confiscated them. Yet they told him that the pants would be used as a pattern, that Orderville pants would be styled after them, and that he'd get the first pair.

What President Eyring called "The pants rebellion" did not end there. The factory was now swamped with orders for new pants, but those orders were denied because the pants weren't worn out enough, which began a rash of pants wearing out prematurely, such as when boys would sneak into the shed where the grinding wheel was housed to do a number on their pants. Eventually, the leaders of the order "gave in, sent a load of wool out to trade for cloth, and the new-style pants were produced for everyone," Eyring said, explaining that it wasn't the happiest of endings because Orderville residents suffered from the problem of not remembering their struggles in the Muddy Mission.

Besides envy and an improving local economy, there were other factors that led to the Order's demise. One was that the Order's biggest champion, Brigham Young, died in 1877, and his successors were not as encouraging. The equal wages and other factors also led to internal disunion, and members of the younger generation became disenchanted, feeling they would not have equal stock in the organization. The Order tried to address the wage problem and restructure its system to pay skilled laborers more than unskilled laborers, but even Apostle Erastus Snow, who was not a huge advocate of the Order himself, said doing so was, in essence, giving into selfishness.

Another contributing factor that became a chink in the communal system's armor was the destruction of the dining hall by flood in 1880, meaning the families of the order no longer sat together to eat.

The Edmunds Act of 1882, which made polygamy a felony, also helped signal the Order's death knell as many of its members practiced polygamy, chief among them was Thomas Chamberlain, the order's dynamic leader. Some members fled to escape capture, and some were apprehended and served jail time, including Chamberlain. The end came in 1885 when most of the organization's assets were sold at auction, with former members doing their best to get their property back. Ever since, Orderville's residents were left to fend for themselves in a capitalistic economy, just like the citizens of all the neighboring towns.

Unfortunately, very little in Orderville remains to remind residents and visitors of the town's interesting history. The biggest reminder is the Daughters of Utah Pioneers Museum, whose structure is built from stone from the schoolhouse built just after the United Order disbanded. The museum displays pictures of United Order members and their families as well as time-period clothing and tools, but few actual relics used by United Order members survive, admits museum guide, Colene Brinkerhoff.

Connie Goulding, who wrote a short book about the town's history for sale at the museum entitled *How Orderville Got its Name*, said it's a shame there isn't more to remind today's residents and visitors of the town's storied past, and that's one of the reasons she wrote her book. She said expressly that she wrote it so her children and grandchildren could pass down those stories.

Tourists, who are absolutely vital to Orderville's economy, pass through and just think it's a town with a weird name without knowing the story behind it, Goulding said. Goulding, along with her sister and brother-in-law, Donna and Brad Adair, are trying to remedy that.

Ten years ago, the Adairs purchased the town's old Zion's Cooperative Mercantile Institution building, which was built just after the Order ended and had fallen into complete disrepair, along with the building next to it, a former grocery store. They turned the grocery store into the Soup Town Cafe, a charming eatery that serves soups (obviously), sandwiches, and ice cream. They restored the old ZCMI building at their own expense and have turned it into a private museum (free of charge) that displays photographs of the United Order period as well as a few relics of the time period. The centerpiece is a model recreating what Orderville looked like during its heyday—row houses around a square with a common dining hall fashioned by noted artist Elbert Porter from a sketch of the United Order's town layout. Goulding said the model, commissioned by the town in 1976 for its July 24 celebration, had gone back and forth from place to place for a while but now has found a permanent home.

The Adairs have tried to get the old ZCMI building on the National Register of Historic Places but failed because it had been "too cut up," Goulding said, and someday hope to establish a park behind the Co-op building with historical markings explaining the Order's history.

The Daughters of Utah Pioneers Museum in Orderville displays artifacts used by United Order members and other period items

Visiting Orderville

Only twenty-one miles north of Kanab on U.S. Highway 89, Orderville's central location makes a great base camp for visiting the area's national parks, including Zion, Cedar Breaks, Bryce Canyon and the North Rim of the Grand Canyon.

An Orderville itinerary, as mentioned previously, should include a stop at the DUP Museum next to the elementary school, which is open Friday from 2 p.m. to 4 p.m., Saturday 11 a.m. to 2 p.m. or by appointment, and the old ZCMI building with its model of how the town looked during its United Order days. Another curiosity Goulding recommends is The Rock Stop, a gift shop that resembles a large rock complete with a waterfall at its entrance fashioned by Porter, the same artist who created the model on display at the ZCMI building.

And while there, try to imagine what life would have been like in the town when all things were held in common with neighbors.

Would that have been a utopia or a dystopia?

The original story and photo gallery can be found at the following link:

https://www.stgeorgeutah.com/news/
archive/2019/07/28/united-order-day-
southern-utahs-version-of-communism/

FOR FURTHER INFORMATION
Visit Southern Utah's Orderville web page

https://visitsouthernutah.com/
communities/orderville/

The Parowan Gap is identified by a Bureau of Land
Management sign when approaching it from the west

12

THE PAROWAN GAP
Interpretations and Mysteries of a Petroglyph Heaven

One of the most concentrated collections of Native American petroglyphs in the Western United States—and also one of the least understood—is in Southern Utah's backyard: the Parowan Gap.

The Native Americans who etched these images into the rock held it in high regard, as do their descendants today.

"It's a peaceful site, a sacred site," said Dave Jacobsen, Bureau of Land Management Cedar City Field Office outdoor recreation director. "There is a unique feeling to it."

According to archaeologists, people have been living in the area surrounding the Parowan Gap for over twelve thousand years. The first inhabitants were hunters and gatherers, moving with the seasons.

Few artifacts remain of these ancient people, and archaeologists believe that the people responsible for most of the rock art lived during what is known as the Fremont period, starting at about 500 A.D. These people may have lived just east of the Gap, living in pit-houses, growing staple crops such as corn and making pottery.

However, excavations of the site have shown no evidence to suggest that ancient people lived near the Gap long term, BLM Cedar City Field Office archaeologist Jamie Palmer said. They probably stayed for a couple of days and then moved on.

The ancient population passing through wanted to put their mark on the place.

"They followed the animals and the seasons," said Dorena Martineau, cultural resources director of the Paiute Indian Tribe of Utah.

Given the petroglyphs' abstract nature, nothing sticks out to give archaeologists a firm idea as to when they were inscribed, Palmer said.

Regardless of their date, the Gap's petroglyphs tell countless stories of the people who etched the rock art itself, of the plants and animals of the area, and also of the formation of the Gap.

"Even though we can't read the petroglyphs, they're important stories from our past, small and big," Martineau said. "It's like our library."

The Gap's petroglyph gallery includes over ninety panels and approximately fifteen hundred figures of varied subjects, including lizards, snakes, human figures, bear claws, mountain sheep, and even geometric designs.

The challenge is the interpretation of these stories displayed in stone for thousands of years. For instance, some interpret cross-shaped images as birds either in flight or making tracks along the ground. This depiction matches up with the bird habitat around the Gap today, where birds of prey such as golden eagles, peregrine falcons, prairie falcons, red-tailed hawks, and great-horned owls nest.

The most unique rock art at the Gap is what is known as the "zipper glyph." While the other rock art in the Gap isn't necessarily one-of-a-kind, there is nothing like the zipper glyph seen anywhere else. And it is a prime example of the differences in interpretation of the Gap petroglyphs. In the astro-archaeological perspective, the zipper is a map of the site, showing how the solstices and equinoxes align with it.

However, according to the Paiute Tribe, the glyph is about a man's journey and a few other events, such as people starving.

"It's a map of where they had gone," Martineau said of the zipper glyph with its corresponding marks all the way around.

One of the fun things each visitor gets to do is interpret the petroglyphs him or herself, Palmer said, but probably no one will ever know what they truly mean.

"We're not likely to understand it anytime soon," he said.

The BLM has provided an attractive viewing area for visitors inspecting the "zipper glyph" at the Parowan Gap

From Then Until Now

The Parowan Gap is made of Navajo sandstone and started forming approximately two hundred million years ago when sand dunes covered much of the area. Many other layers of sediment compressed, uplifted, and faulted to expose the layer of stone. It is known as a wind gap because the ancient river that carved it no longer runs through it, drying up possibly when the climate grew hotter and drier.

The first recorded mention of the Parowan Gap was in the journal of Robert Campbell, clerk and historian of an exploring expedition that broke off from a larger group led by Parley P. Pratt, an early apostle of The Church of Jesus Christ of Latter-day Saints.

Campbell copied some of the petroglyphs into two pages of his journal. Upon returning to Salt Lake City, Pratt told Brigham Young that Ute Indian leader Chief Walker called the Parowan Gap "God's Own House."

One of the most interesting aspects of the Gap's history is the transformation over the years both of the site itself and its interpretation. Better interpretation, aesthetics, and different perspectives were at the core of a BLM upgrade of the site in 2013.

For years, there was a chain-link fence as a barrier between visitors and the petroglyphs with a three-panel kiosk in the dirt parking lot, providing the interpretation of the rock art.

One of the disadvantages of this arrangement was aesthetics, but the main problem was that visitors were receiving no chance themselves to view the interpretation in close proximity to the actual petroglyphs. Either the visitor would read about the rock art on the interpretive panels, then go see the petroglyphs, or look at the rock art first, then read about it.

The BLM observed that people interacting with the site seemed confused. When considering changes to the site, the BLM wanted to ensure it meshed well, and with the help of a landscape architect, they did their best to put together the best interactive flow.

Another problem with the previous setup was that visitors were only getting one side of the story: the astro-archaeological perspective of archaeologists who have researched the Gap. There was no perspective of the Paiute Tribe, the descendants of the native peoples who etched the art into the stone thousands of years ago.

"The tribe really wanted their voice heard," Palmer said, adding that the BLM approached the tribe in 2003 about changing the interpretation of the site.

Martineau said she appreciates the BLM's efforts on behalf of the tribe and that the tribe has a great relationship with the agency.

Today, interpretive panels—several with the Paiute perspective next to the astro-archaeological perspective—stand near the petroglyphs. More attractive, less imposing steel fences were erected between the visitor area and the rock art.

Jacobsen said he thinks there is a night-and-day difference in what the site looks like now compared to what it used to be. There is no more confusion among visitors.

Before the placement of the new interpretive materials, Jacobsen said, people didn't know where to go, but now they know where to go intuitively.

"It just draws you into it," he said, adding that visitor survey data regarding the improvements has been positive.

Another advantage of the new interpretive materials is awareness of the nearby dinosaur tracks. Before the new interpretation, mostly only locals knew about the nearby dinosaur tracks. There was no interpretation at the site and a lot of trash, Jacobsen said. Now they know it's there, they can learn more about it, and they respect it.

The new improvements have also helped somewhat with vandalism, which has been a problem at the Gap since early settlers discovered it. Today, pioneer inscriptions on the rock have become part of the historical record, but in general, defacing the rock art or putting one's own mark on the stone is an offense punishable by law.

Jacobsen said vandalism has decreased at the site since the installation of the new fences and interpretive panels, but unfortunately it hasn't ceased completely. There were bullet holes in some of the interpretive panels before new ones were ordered and placed just in time for the Summer Solstice event.

Defacing aside, visitors are asked to not even touch the petroglyphs, Martineau said, because the oils from their skin can harm them.

Fun Historic Stops in Southern Utah

In addition to the better physical interpretation at the site, the BLM has started to promote the Gap in other ways. It recently revamped its web pages that discuss the Gap. Part of the interpretation on the website includes interviews with Paiute tribal elders.

Palmer said that they want to promote it better, tell the story and let people know it's for everyone, not just for Iron County.

A petroglyph panel on the Parowan Gap's south side reveals large ancient inscriptions with circular and rectangular patterns

Visiting the Parowan Gap

To get to the Parowan Gap, drive north on State Route 130 (accessed from Interstate 15's Exit 62) approximately 17.3 miles and turn right on 12800 North.

There is a sign clearly labeling the turnoff to the Gap, which is only 2.4 miles after you turn. Park in the parking lot to the left after driving through the Gap itself.

For the full experience, walk the pathways on both sides of the road and read the interpretive signs at each set of petroglyphs and points of interest.

The dinosaur tracks are a nice supplement to the petroglyphs—a stroll through what feels like a rock garden with birds of prey nesting above.

Summer Solstice Event Details

Solstice and equinox parties, the Summer Solstice, one, in particular, are the most popular events at the Gap. Hosted by the Parowan Heritage Foundation with permission from the BLM, the Solstice event allows visitors to see the summer sun line up perfectly with the Gap.

"It's pretty spectacular," Jacobsen said.

Because of this ideal alignment, some say the Parowan Gap serves as a calendar, but that's the white man's perspective, Jacobsen said, adding that the tribe doesn't feel it's a calendar.

The original story and photo gallery can be found at the following link:

https://www.stgeorgeutah.com/news/
archive/2019/06/16/raw-petroglyph-day-
interpretations-and-mysteries-of-parowan-
gap/

FOR FURTHER INFORMATION
Parowan City's Parowan Gap web page

https://parowan.org/parowan-gap/

*The Old Sorrel Monument, located by the
America First Events Center, is a noticeable reminder of
Southern Utah University's faith-promoting past*

13

SOUTHERN UTAH UNIVERSITY
A Faith-Promoting Founding and a
Symbol of Community Spirit

It was once known as a "normal school," but its foundation story is anything but.

Southern Utah University stands today as a "striking example of the extent of the commitment of Utah's early pioneers to the cause of education," the plaque on campus detailing the school's foundation story reads.

The reminders of the school's inspiring past are ubiquitous, from monuments on campus to the rhetoric of the school's administration and faculty leaders, and that's a good thing.

The Faith-Promoting Founding

During its first full session after becoming a state in 1896, the Utah State Legislature authorized a branch of the state's teacher training school to be located in Southern Utah. The main requirement for the community chosen was to deed the state fifteen acres of land and construct on that site, a college building designed by the state architect.

Beaver and Cedar City were the top contenders, with Parowan and Paragonah also considered.

"Cedar City's citizens sought the selection with great fervor and organization. The city's fine educational record was in its favor, as was its central location in Southern Utah," Janet Burton Seegmiller wrote in her book *A History of Iron County: Community Above Self*.

Another advantage Cedar City had was that the town did not have a saloon, a claim none of the other communities in contention could make.

When it won the bid, Cedar City had a population of fewer than fifteen hundred residents. It gave the state title to Academy Hill, the present site of the upper campus, but concluded that the town did not have the means to construct the building the state required. Instead, the community decided to utilize an existing building downtown, Ward Hall, which was still under construction.

Classes started at the Branch Normal School (BNS) in September 1897, with Milton Bennion as principal and Howard R. Driggs, Annie Spencer, and George W. Decker as teachers, according to Seegmiller.

At first, this arrangement seemed to be working. Only two months into the first term's classes, however, the Utah Attorney General refused the teachers' payrolls, saying that the community had not complied with the state mandate, which required that the school have its own building on the land deeded to the state. At that point, the state gave Cedar City an ultimatum; if it didn't build a structure on that deeded land by September 1898, it would lose its school. To resolve the issue, three Cedar City families secured a bank loan by mortgaging their homes to ensure the teachers were paid.

Constructing the building proved to be more difficult.

"The cost of building was equivalent to the town's total business volume for an entire year and would require bucking the mountain snows to construct the new building," the foundation story plaque on campus reads. "A building committee was appointed to which Cedar City pledged all its public and private resources, the committee being forced to dip into both generously."

The community banded together and started gathering materials for the BNS building on Academy Hill. They started making bricks, quarrying sandstone and sawing lumber on Cedar Mountain and hauling it to town, but an early fall snowstorm shut down the operation, Seegmiller wrote. Due to these initial difficulties in construction, Bennion traveled to Salt Lake City to meet with the Utah Board of Regents and ask for an extension of the deadline, but the board wouldn't budge.

On New Year's Day, 1898, Cedar City residents met to create a plan of attack, ultimately deciding that they were willing to try to get lumber from Heber Jensen's sawmill at Mammoth Creek before the snow started to melt.

"Nothing so hazardous had ever been purposefully undertaken in Iron County," Seegmiller wrote.

In her book, *Southern Utah University: The First 100 Years*, Anne Leavitt wrote that residents realized if they waited until spring, they might be bogged down by mud or be too busy farming to make much of an effort. This contingent of brave men, none of whom would actually attend the school being built, decided it was best to make the attempt in winter when they did not have to worry about their crops.

A resident by the name of Neil Bladen led the expedition, in which they loaded the lumber from Mammoth Creek onto wagons and headed back to Cedar City. They had to leave the lumber on their wagons, however, because they were buried in snow after the first night's camp.

"Howling winds had shaped the loose snow into drifts ten to fifteen feet deep and seventy-five to one hundred yards long," Seegmiller wrote.

It was in this tough situation that one of the most celebrated heroes of the school's founding emerged.

He was a "big, rangy, 8-year-old draft horse, called Sorrel because of his color," Leavitt wrote. "He was from Percheron grandsire, strong and steady. Described as 'long-legged, long-necked and long-faced,' he weighed about 1,600 pounds. ... His reaction to the crisis was markedly different from other horses."

While other horses worked the drifts and struggled to keep their noses above the snow, Old Sorrel "pushed and strained against the drifts until they gave way," then "worked at the drifts until the wagons were out of danger," Seegmiller wrote.

The operation was almost called off after this first try, but the community worked together to support the mountain crew bringing the lumber down, dividing the thirty-mile trip from the sawmill to Cedar City into four segments.

"Men made bobsleds or sleighs, and women made sheepskin-lined coats, long underwear and caps with ear protectors," Seegmiller wrote.

Even regular snowstorms and temperatures reaching 40 degrees below zero did not stop the operation, which fortuitously resulted in no serious injuries to the thrity-three men involved and only three horse deaths.

The entire population of the town helped the construction in some way. From cutting stones for the foundation to sharpening tools to providing food for the workmen.

"It is said that women ran the town businesses and other operations while the men were engaged at the school," Seegmiller wrote.

The result of their work is what is now known as Old Main, completed in September 1898. At the time, it was called BNS, and later it was the library. The building was remodeled after a fire in 1948.

In 2003, the building was vacated because of seismic safety and dysfunctional utilities, which led to the raising of funds to save the historic structure. It was remodeled and rededicated in 2008 along with the Carter Carillon and Emma Eccles Jones Education Building constructed next to it.

Fun Historic Stops in Southern Utah

In 2015, SUU communications professor Jon Smith headed up and produced a documentary entitled *Back Up the Mountain* that dramatizes the foundation story, which university leaders and faculty regularly recount today to make connections to the past. The story is a message about the close relationship between the local community and the university, history professor Laura Davis said.

"Without the support and commitment of Cedar City residents, Branch Normal School would have never opened in 1897," Davis explained. "These close ties have continued over the years as both the college and the city grew and expanded. They still remain strong to this day, to the benefit of everyone."

Old Main, renovated in 2008, is still a fixture on the SUU campus

Changing Identities

For the first fifty-six years of its existence, what is now SUU was a branch of another in-state school.

From its founding in 1897 to 1913, it was a branch of the University of Utah and offered high school instruction. Its graduates went on to teach at schools in Southern Utah while some moved on to the college level. As the only state-supported high school in Utah, the BNS continually had to fight for its survival.

Legislators from neighboring counties contended that the state should not maintain a high school in Cedar City while they had to pay for their high schools by means of local taxes and donations, Seegmiller wrote.

Under the auspices of the University of Utah, the normal school could not offer higher education classes, to which Cedar City residents opposed, feeling that was the school's expressed purpose from its founding. In 1913, to rectify the situation, Iron County state representative Wilford Day drove a bill through the legislature that transferred the school from the University of Utah to the Utah State Agricultural College (now Utah State University) in Logan, becoming known by the moniker Branch Agricultural College, or BAC.

However, with this move, Cedar City residents feared that teacher programs would go by the wayside in favor of agricultural programs, but that proved to be unfounded as the school retained its teacher courses and also added science, arts, business, music, and of course, agricultural programs.

For a little over two decades after becoming BAC, the school still taught high school students. That changed in the fall of 1941 when the high school was separated from the college, and all high schoolers were moved to the new Cedar High School.

Predictably, enrollment declined during World War II, and some thought it might signal the end of the college. But former Cedar City Mayor Walter Granger was serving as Utah's congressman at the time, and had a major influence in establishing an air corps training program in Cedar City, which helped keep the school going, Seegmiller wrote.

At the war's end, enrollment hit new highs, and over the next decade, there was an average of four to five hundred students on campus every school year.

One of the challenges during the school's earlier years was providing housing and jobs for its students. Some students were fortunate to live with relatives, and others had parents who moved to Cedar City to give their children the chance to attend school there.

*Letterman sweaters and jackets from the school's
past identities hold a prominent place in the display
cases at the America First Events Center*

"Almost every fall for years, articles in the *Iron County Record* begged members of the community to open their homes to incoming students," Seegmiller wrote.

As enrollment increased rapidly during the post-war years, war surplus buildings, trailers, and barracks from military bases became solutions for housing. At least four buildings from the Topaz Japanese Internment Camp near Delta became student housing.

To Vice President for Alumni and Community Relations Mindy Benson, the BAC was a center of culture and education, not only for Cedar City and Iron County but also for the surrounding communities.

"Alumni who attended the BAC from 1913-1953 have immense pride in the 'Grand Old BAC,' and they truly identified with that institution," Benson said. "I think a lot of history was created during those years of students receiving a quality education with professors who cared and provided personal attention, a hallmark for SUU even today."

In 1953, the era of the BAC came to an end as the school became the College of Southern Utah but was still under the auspices of Utah State University. This title fits more than its previous monikers as seventy-two percent of the students in 1955 came outside of Cedar City, and ninety percent of that number were from Southern Utah. That year, the school had less than fifty faculty and staff members and 427 students. But by 1963, with the first of the baby-boomer generation attending college, enrollment skyrocketed to over one thousand.

Since their school was first established, Cedar City residents had a vision of an independent, four-year higher education institution. And by the late 1950s, the community established a committee, chaired by Dixie Leavitt, to work toward that goal.

After his election to the Utah Legislature, Leavitt went full-throttle on the issue and proposed two bills in the 1965 session, one granting the school the right to confer four-year degrees and the other to separate the school from USU as a new state college.

During the session's last days, it didn't look like these two bills would come up for debate. But Leavitt enlisted the help of Thorpe Waddington, the Senate majority leader from Delta, to get them on the docket. When the two bills came up for debate, they passed unanimously in both the House and the Senate.

"The move to independent status opened the way for growth for the community and the institution that share a unique relationship," Seegmiller wrote. "Under the direction of (Dr. Royden C.) Braithwaite, the institution developed bachelor's degree programs in more than thirty areas in addition to refining vocational programs and offering pre-professional training in dentistry, law, medicine, pharmacology, and veterinary science."

More changes came only four years after independent status, as the school became Southern Utah State College in 1969. By 1980, under the Division of Continuing Education, SUSC began offering classes outside of its main campus in St. George, Kanab, Richfield, and Delta, Seegmiller wrote.

While enrollment growth stagnated in the 1970s, partly due to the lagging local economy, it started growing again after 1981 when alumnus Gerald R. Sherratt took the helm of the college. Under his tenure, The Centrum, known today as the America First Event Center, was built in 1986 as a special events arena that hosts various sports programs, commencement exercises, and other community events. That same year, Sherratt conceived the idea of the Utah Summer Games, a grass-roots Olympic-style sports festival based on campus involving amateur athletes from all over the state.

In 1990, a decision by the Utah Board of Regents and State Legislature completely fulfilled the dream of the community members of the late 19th century. The legislation approved university status, cementing the school's status as a comprehensive four-year institution, turning into what it is today, Southern Utah University.

"I think SUU always had an identity, even prior to its designation as College of Southern Utah," Faculty Senate President and long-time Psychology Professor Steve Barney said. "The Branch Normal School was responsible for educating teachers in this geographic region. That tradition has lived on with our absolute commitment to preparing students to meet the demands and needs of our local, regional, national, and international society."

Community Spirit

Over the course of its history, SUU has shown tremendous community spirit that has culminated in many worthwhile projects.

In the 1950s, the college and community came together to build what was then known as the College Cabin eleven miles up Cedar Canyon from Cedar City. Now known as the SUU Mountain Center, it has gone through remodels and improvements over the years and hosts many college, community, and private events in a picturesque mountain setting.

The school's Ashcroft Observatory is another example of the college and community working together on a worthwhile project. Opened in the 1970s, the observatory sits on a hill west of town and provides the opportunity for community members and school groups to learn about constellations and distant parts of the galaxy.

Many students find out about SUU through their experience attending one of the plays or workshops offered every year by the Utah Shakespeare Festival.

The Adams Theatre, built in the late 1970s, is patterned after the outdoor Globe Theatre where Shakespeare's plays were performed during the playwright's lifetime

Benson shared the story of a current SUU gymnast who, in an Instagram post, said that attending the Shakespeare Festival has been life-changing and a true joy, noting that all of her worries disappear as soon as she steps into one of its theaters.

"The festival is an important part of outside perceptions of SUU and Cedar City in general," SUU history professor Mark Miller said. "It brings in a lot of talent and outside energy to the campus, especially when students come for competitions, and people come to stay during the summer to attend the plays."

Founded in 1962 by theater professor Fred Adams, the festival has grown from a small all-volunteer operation to a large non-profit arts organization with state-of-the-art facilities that attract nearly one hundred thousand patrons who view almost three hundred plays each year.

The Southern Utah Museum of Art (SUMA) is one of the most recent additions to the University's community offerings. Opened in 2016, the museum displays the artwork of regional landscape artists, SUU faculty, and student artists, as well as other distinguished artists from around the country.

Fun Historic Stops in Southern Utah

SUU sponsors seventeen NCAA Division 1 athletic teams, seven men's sports, and ten women's sports, who compete in the Big Sky Conference. Known as the Thunderbirds today, the school's mascot, just like its name, has gone through a few changes over the years. The mascot was first known as the Aggies, to honor its parent school, and then the Broncos.

One of the most enjoyable things to do on campus is simply to stroll through it and take in its beauty with its mix of historic and modern buildings, fountains, waterfalls, and native trees set in groves along pathways with benches. A statue immortalizing the efforts of Old Sorrel stands near the America First Event Center, and the Sharwan Smith Student Center displays the "rescue wagon" used to get that integral lumber down the mountain to build the community's beloved school.

The original story and photo gallery can be found at the following link:

https://www.stgeorgeutah.com/news/archive/2019/08/25/raw-suu-history-day-a-faith-promoting-founding-and-a-symbol-of-community-spirit/

FOR FURTHER INFORMATION
Southern Utah University history web page:

https://www.suu.edu/general/history.html

The Topaz Museum in downtown Delta tells the story of Japanese Americans relocated to the Utah desert during World War II

14

TOPAZ INTERNMENT CAMP
The Sobering Story of Utah's Version of the World War II Concentration Camp

When one thinks of concentration camps, what usually comes to mind are the Nazi Germany camps of World War II, but what many may not realize is that the United States had its own version of concentration camps during that era, and one was situated in central Utah.

The camps in Nazi Germany cannot be forgotten: They implemented what was called the Final Solution to the "Jewish problem." They used gas chambers to eliminate those unfit to work and treated those fit to work worse than the slaves of the antebellum South; they were collectively known for the Holocaust, leading to the death of approximately six million Jews and others their perpetrators considered undesirable.

Fun Historic Stops in Southern Utah

While nearly nothing like the Nazi camps and lacking such an evil purpose, a United States version of concentration camps— some top government brass (including President Franklin D. Roosevelt himself) even called them that—did exist. Their aim, however, wasn't to eliminate people; their aim was to keep a watchful eye on an entire race—those of Japanese ancestry— approximately two-thirds of whom were American citizens. They were known more formally as internment camps or the more euphemistic "relocation centers."

The Central Utah War Relocation Center was established northeast of Delta, called Topaz after a nearby mountain.

America's internment camps affected approximately one hundred twenty thousand people on the West Coast. Thankfully, very few died in the camps. But even though the camps were distinctly different from their German counterparts, to many, what happened in the internment camps cannot be easily excused and swept under the rug. The camps took away residents' basic civil and constitutional rights in the name of national defense while in reality—particularly in hindsight—they may represent a bad case of war hysteria.

There were rumors of sabotage with practically no distinction made between Japanese nationals and Japanese immigrants living in the U.S. with their citizen children.

"Ironically—though this mass incarceration was provoked by accusations of disloyalty—not a single Japanese American was prosecuted or convicted for any instance of espionage toward the United States," the Topaz Museum brochure states.

Minister Truman B. Douglass wrote in a 1944 pamphlet:

"This did not occur in a foreign country under tyrannical dictatorship, 70,000 American Refugees Made in USA. . . . It happened in America under the flag, which stands for 'liberty and justice for all'."

The Executive Order

In the wake of the attack on Pearl Harbor, on February 19, 1942, under pressure from within and without his administration,

President Roosevelt signed Executive Order 9066, which authorized the relocation of Americans of Japanese ancestry to ten camps across the Western United States to ensure they didn't do anything to aid the Japanese government as they feared they might.

Just as the U.S. Constitution does not include the word "slavery," the words "Japanese" or "Japan" were not included in the order, but everyone knew to what people the edict referred.

Without any hearings or trials, these Japanese-Americans were given short notice—some only days—to prepare to leave the life they had known for so long for the unknown. Most did not even know where they were going as they boarded the trains to leave. They could only take what they could carry, meaning that many of them had to sell high-value possessions, such as homes and cars, at fire-sale prices. Partly due to the loyalty infused in their culture, most didn't put up a fuss and left without any strife, staying in the camps with patient resignation waiting for the day they would be free to build their own lives where they wanted to again.

*A flagpole and some monuments stand as reminders of the
Topaz Japanese Internment Camp*

Topaz Daily Life

Topaz opened on September 11, 1942, upon the arrival of trains carrying five hundred internees and fifty military guards after long trips in which they were packed in rail cars like sardines. Most came from the San Francisco area and, prior to their arrival at Topaz, were incarcerated at the Tanforan Race Track in San Bruno, California, forced to live in horse stalls until Topaz was completed.

Topaz housed 11,212 residents during its short stint, and its peak population was about eighty-one hundred. Topaz was its own enclosed city—the fifth largest in the state at the time—during its just more than three-year existence.

When the first batch of people arrived, not everything was finished.

"Once at the Topaz location, some internees were hired to finish building their own barracks, put up the barbed wire fence, and complete other structures at the site," the museum's history page notes.

The camp included forty-two blocks; the first few were the administration buildings, warehouses, and government workers housing with the remaining blocks housing residents. Each block included twelve apartment buildings, a recreation hall, men's and women's latrines, and a mess hall. Each building was sectioned off into six apartments of different sizes to accommodate families.

Families lived in one-room barrack-style housing that "were little more than pine planks covered with tar paper on the outside and sheetrock on the inside," one museum interpretive panel notes. In each room were four army cots without mattresses, a coal stove, a light bulb, and two army blankets per person. Many internees built additional furniture from scrap wood.

The crowded spaces ranged from twenty feet by fourteen feet for two people to twenty feet by twenty-six feet for a family of six. The barracks had no running water or insulation, and during windstorms, dust found its way in through the doors, walls, and windows even though rags and wet newspapers were stuffed in the cracks.

Families tried to make the best of the situation. Adults had jobs that paid them a pittance (wages ranged from $12-$19 a month) but soldiered on. Children went to school at one of two elementary schools or the junior-senior high school. Some residents even cultivated their own gardens.

Even in such conditions, 136 couples were married in Topaz; their courtships consisted of more mundane things such as sharing tomato soup around a pot-bellied stove or watching a movie in the recreation hall. They had to travel to Fillmore, the county seat fifty-four miles away, just to get a marriage license.

Anna Towata, who was one of those Topaz brides, wrote that she cried on her first anniversary because all it consisted of was going to a mess hall for dinner and then going to another mess hall for a movie, according to one of the museum's interpretive panels.

"This is no first anniversary," she complained to her husband, who responded, "Don't worry, there'll be other anniversaries." And there were—forty-nine of them.

Topaz youth went to school just like anyone else, but it was more difficult for them to be motivated under their circumstances. A War Relocation Authority report about Topaz in 1944 even noted that Topaz students showed an attitude of resignation and apathy toward the future, a museum interpretive panel notes, but the students' teachers, both Japanese and American, encouraged them to never give up.

"I never ceased to have a lump in my throat when classes recited the Pledge of Allegiance, especially the phrase 'liberty and justice for all,'" said Eleanor Gerard Sekerak, who was a student at Topaz.

Once in a while, however, Topaz students did have something to be proud of and to keep them going, such as when the Topaz football team defeated Millard High School November 11, 1943.

Art was an escape for Topaz internees, both youth and adults alike. They sculpted wood into smooth shapes or gathered shells to make delicate jewelry and even dolls. Others expressed themselves through traditional dance, flower arranging, music, and poetry.

Internees published a daily newspaper called *The Topaz Times* and issues of a literary arts magazine called *TREK* and a similar one called *All Aboard*.

"On the surface, the paintings, drawings, and artwork from

Japanese Americans at Topaz may look pleasant," a museum interpretive panel says, but looking closer at them, they feature guard towers and barbed wire and serve as a sort-of diary. "The art produced at Topaz is some of the most powerful to come out of the WRA camps."

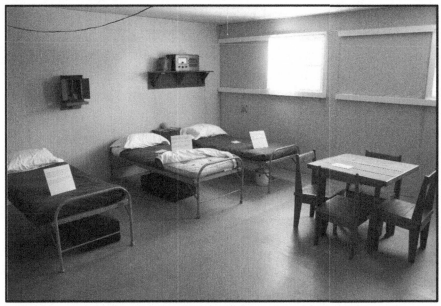

This recreation of the Topaz Relocation Center barracks provides museum visitors a glimpse into how Japanese-American internees lived during World War II

The Camp's End

In early 1943, the War Department and the WRA required everyone in internment camps that was seventeen or older to take a loyalty questionnaire.

"The questions, focusing on their religion, language, and club memberships, caught Japanese-Americans off guard," a museum interpretive panel states. "Some questions were confusing, others seemed like entrapment."

Anyone deemed disloyal—and there were fourteen hundred of them at Topaz—was sent to a high-security camp at Tule Lake in Northern California. For some, saying "no" to certain questions on the form wasn't a matter of loyalty, but one of protest.

The questionnaire did lead to internees around the nation being drafted into or volunteering for the U.S. Army. The irony is these former internees were fighting for a country that stood for freedom but still incarcerated their families. These young Japanese-Americans from the internment camps joined the 442nd Regimental Combat Team in Europe, the museum brochure states, which became the U.S. Army's most highly decorated unit for its size and duration of service.

One of the most unfortunate incidents to occur at Topaz was the shooting death of sixty-three-year-old James Wakasa by one of the Topaz guards on April 11, 1943. The guard gave no warning shot and claimed Wakasa was trying to escape. The death caused quite a stir with internees fearing they would be targeted by "Jap-hating guards," and Japanese leaders demanded they be part of the investigation. The guard was tried but let off. After the shooting, however, policies relaxed, and soldiers in the guard tower were removed during daylight hours.

After Topaz closed in October 1945, people from all over Utah bought and removed its buildings for use as houses and farm buildings. Half a barrack sold for $250. For instance, Delta farmer Eldro Jeffery purchased half a barrack that once served as a Boy Scout meeting hall; his family donated it to the Great Basin Museum in 1991, and the Topaz Museum Board later restored it to its 1943 appearance as an exhibit for the museum.

The Apology

A presidential commission investigated the incarceration of Japanese-Americans in the early 1980s. At the time of incarceration, the action was implemented without a dissenting vote, but looking back, hindsight is truly 20/20.

"The promulgation of Executive Order 9066 was not justified by military necessity, and the decisions which followed from it—detention, ending detention, and ending exclusion—were not driven by analysis of military conditions," the presidential commission's report stated. "The broad historical causes which shaped these decisions were race prejudice, war hysteria, and a failure of political leadership."

For years after the camps were closed, Japanese-American groups sought an apology and redress from the government. That finally came when Congress passed the Civil Liberties Act of 1988, which acknowledged it had violated internees' basic civil liberties and constitutional rights. The act authorized payments of $20,000 to each living camp survivor, more than eighty-two thousand of them. Unfortunately, the apology came too late for nearly forty thousand.

"A monetary sum and words alone cannot restore lost years or erase painful memories; neither can they fully convey our Nation's resolve to rectify injustice and to uphold the rights of individuals," read President George Bush's apology letter that accompanied the redress checks.

"We can never fully right the wrongs of the past," Bush's letter continued. "But we can take a clear stand for justice and recognize that serious injustices were done to Japanese-Americans during World War II. In enacting a law calling for restitution and offering a sincere apology, your fellow Americans have, in a very real sense, renewed their traditional commitment to the ideals of freedom, equality, and justice."

That 1988 legislation also made it okay to talk about the internment camps, and their story began to find its way into the country's historical narrative as well as become part of the curriculum for U.S. history courses.

The Museum

In 1976, Japanese American Citizen League chapters from Salt Lake City erected a monument near the site of the former Topaz camp.

The Topaz Museum Board was established in 1997 as a nonprofit organization with the avowed mission to preserve the history of Topaz Camp. In 1999, the board began purchasing land of the former Topaz camp site and to date owns 626 acres of its original six hundred forty acres.

The National Park Service named the site a national historic landmark in 2007, and by 2011, the board possessed eighty-seven paintings done at the Topaz Art School. The board received park service Japanese-American Confinement Sites grants and raised additional funds to construct the museum, which was finished in 2014. It opened in 2015, first displaying the Topaz art.

The grand opening of the museum exhibits recounting the history of the Topaz Internment Camp, followed from July 7-8, 2017.

The Topaz Museum features numerous displays that tell the story of daily life in the former relocation camp, including this one about the camp's newspaper

Visiting Topaz

The Topaz Museum is located at 55 W. Main St., Delta, next door to the Great Basin Museum.

At the museum, visitors can watch two short videos, one containing excerpts of home videos taken by Topaz internee Dave Tatsuno and another about the camp's history. The informative museum displays depict daily life in the camps with poignant pictures and artifacts, show a recreation of one of the barrack living quarters and the restored recreation hall in the back of the museum.

The museum, open Mondays through Saturdays from 10 a.m. to 5 p.m., provides visitors a copy of a map with directions to the actual Topaz site as well as an information sheet detailing where some of the former barracks currently reside in Delta. Since the camp's buildings were sold and carted off to other places, the site itself contains only a few remnants of the actual camp, including building foundations, a coal chute, and a few other odds and ends. An Eagle Scout project installed signs showing where former camp buildings once stood as well as markers denoting the location of each numbered block.

Even though there isn't much there anymore, visiting the actual site is a must for visitors—an eye-opening reminder of what conditions were like for these unfortunate people who left real life behind for a manufactured life in Utah's barren desert.

It also is a reminder that a nation built on freedom should never curtail its citizens' basic human rights in such a manner again.

The original story and photo gallery can be found at the following link:

https://www.stgeorgeutah.com/news/archive/2018/07/15/raw-topaz-history-day-the-sobering-story-of-utahs-concentration-camp/

FOR FURTHER INFORMATION
Topaz Museum website:

http://www.topazmuseum.org/

*The Utah Territorial Statehouse Museum was the only wing
constructed of a plan for a much more grandiose building*

15

UTAH TERRITORIAL STATEHOUSE
Fillmore's Ill-fated Mid 19th-Century
Decision is Now a Historic Jewel

Most drivers on Interstate 15 probably have noticed signs
accompanying the Fillmore exits informing them that a building
in the town of twenty-five hundred residents approximately
halfway between St. George and Salt Lake City once served an
important purpose in Utah's history, but few of them stop to check
it out.

For a few years, believe it or not, Fillmore was the official
capital of Utah—a Utah very different than the one today.

The whole reason for the settlement of Fillmore in October
1851 was to eventually turn it into the seat of government for the
newly-recognized territory. Brigham Young, both president of
The Church of Jesus Christ of Latter-day Saints and governor of

the Utah Territory at the time, foresaw what was then known as Pahvant Valley as a major population center. He chose the site of the future city because it was smack dab in the middle of the territory, whose boundaries back then encompassed most of what is now the state of Nevada.

A few months before the town's establishment, anti-Mormon U.S. President Zachary Taylor had died, leaving Millard Fillmore, his vice president, as his successor. The new president was much more kind toward the Mormons, and his administration approved Utah's drive to become a territory not too long after assuming the presidential mantle.

As a "gift" to the new president, Young selected Fillmore as the name for the town and Millard as the moniker for the county, which at that time extended all the way to the California border. The adulation worked, apparently, since the Fillmore administration appropriated $20,000 to build a capitol building in Fillmore, albeit the amount was less than appropriations given to other territories.

One can only assume that Fillmore's first settlers were brimming with optimism at the prospect of establishing such an important place. An assignment to settle in Millard County might have been seen as much more desirable than a call to a more barren, farther-flung location. Carl Camp, Territorial Statehouse State Park manager, however, said there really is no record describing how any of them felt when they first arrived.

Establishing a new settlement so late in the year definitely had its disadvantages. Many first-year settlers spent the winter in their wagons and/or built quick cabins using cottonwood logs.

The original design for the statehouse, drawn up by Truman O. Angell, architect for the Salt Lake Temple and Young's brother-in-law, envisioned a grand four-winged structure with a domed cupola in the middle. To say it didn't quite work out as planned is a major understatement.

Unfavorable weather, trouble with Native Americans, lack of decent transportation, and squabbling over funding all took their toll and slowed the construction schedule. Another big issue that had to be addressed was building an approximately six-mile road up Chalk Creek to a quarry where sandstone could be easily cut for the building's walls.

Started in 1851, it took until 1854 just to finish the basement. There were questions as to whether Brigham Young was using the appropriations for the building to pay off church debts. Young swore that all of the government funds he received went toward that south wing and later petitioned for more money to complete the whole building as planned, but, unsurprisingly, it was not granted—one of the first indications of the failure that loomed.

Working at a breakneck pace compared to early construction, the stonework for the other two floors went up in three months, and it took a full year to complete the interior, Camp noted. The building was completed in time for the territory's Legislature to meet in late 1855 in what was just the south wing of the building originally planned.

"The early settlers worked long hard hours to build it," said Fred Hayes, late director of the Utah State Parks and Recreation Division. Hayes spent the early part of his career at the State-house.

This rendering of the Utah Territorial Capitol shows a tremendous four-wing edifice that was never completed

"They were pretty proud of their efforts, and many even carved initials and symbols in the stonework," he said. "It kind of became a symbol of their struggle to make something out of nothing, which in reality is the story of the early settlers of the Utah Territory."

That December 1855-January 1856 session was the only full legislative session held in the building. Brigham Young and legislators quickly realized that the distance from the real population center, what was then known as Great Salt Lake City, approximately one hundred fifty miles north, was too much (it often took four days to travel to or from Fillmore) and the small town was not fit to temporarily accommodate all the members of the Legislature.

One good thing the Statehouse brought the town was an excellent venue for dances. Even before the building was finished, settlers regularly held dances that lasted until midnight. One early teacher, Emily Hoyt, wrote in her journal about her displeasure with the late dances because the participants were regularly tired the next day.

Once the Statehouse was finished, a dance was held in celebration before that first legislative session started. Camp said Hoyt disparaged the dances until she got invited to "the big one" to celebrate the opening of the building, a dance in which Brigham Young himself participated.

Besides hosting the Legislature, the building did become the hiding place and base of operations for the *Deseret News* for a few months during the Utah War, when, in 1857, President James Buchanan sent troops led by General Albert Sidney Johnston to supposedly quell what was perceived as a Mormon insurrection against the government.

An extremely short session in 1858 was the last time the building was used by the Legislature. The sole purpose of that meeting was to assemble in what was still legally recognized as the territorial capital to vote to officially move the capital back to Salt Lake City to appease the new federally-appointed governor.

Camp thinks that once early Fillmore settlers realized their town would not be the capital anymore, they were disappointed, he said. Some settlers moved on even if only as far as Meadow a few miles south to start farming.

"I can't imagine the disappointment when the Territorial Statehouse was abandoned literally before it was finished," Hayes said. "I'm sure those masons, carpenters, and others who worked so hard were totally devastated. But, they moved on and made other significant contributions to settlements elsewhere. I think there is a metaphor in there for us all."

The upper room of the Utah Territorial Statehouse served as the venue for legislative meetings and dances

A Host For 'Odds and Ends'

After its short-lived stint as the territory's capitol, the Territorial Statehouse served many different purposes, mainly as a school and a social hall. One of the schools in the building during the 1880s was a Presbyterian Mission School whose main aim was to discourage children from practicing polygamy in the future. It didn't quite achieve that goal, but at least it gave the children a good education.

"It hosted lots of odds and ends," Camp said of the structure, adding that it served as a jail, law offices, library, photography studio, and a hall for the American Legion, which was the only organization on record during that time period to make any improvements to the building—adding another layer to the floor on the top story in 1917.

After the turn of the 20th century, the building fell into disrepair. Just over thirty years after its construction, the Presbyterian Mission School complained about the need to replace some windows and repaint in some places. Later on, local children would crawl in the broken windows and use the basement as a hideout. Considered for demolition, the Daughters of Utah Pioneers stepped in to stop any such thought in 1928.

Not wanting to see the important historical relic gone forever, the organization approached the state to fund the renovation. When it came to the DUP member who was a major impetus for the renovation, Mame Dame, and her attempts to get funding, Camp joked that she "didn't hear you when you said no."

With the help of the state, the DUP restored the building and turned it into a museum in 1930. Members of the DUP operated the museum, and the state parks commission paid the bills, which is why it can lay claim to the title of Utah's first state park. Camp said to this day there is confusion as to which collections are the DUP's and which are the state's since they didn't keep good records.

In 1957, the museum fell under the auspices of the newly created State Parks and Recreation Division and has been operated by it ever since.

Later Trials and Threats

Even though the Territorial Statehouse was the state's first government building, the oldest government building still standing west of the Missouri River and the state's first state park, it sometimes hasn't pleased state legislatures, because it does not draw many annual visitors and thus does not make much revenue.

Most state parks are recreation-oriented, and many—especially those that have a reservoir for boating and water sports—actually make the state money.

"Our heritage parks don't ever do that," Camp said. "We're not making the money."

There have been times the legislature has seriously considered closing the statehouse because they've felt like it's a drain on the State Parks and Recreation Division's budget.

In the late 1990s, one legislator even joked that the park would do better if a representative stood outside the building and handed out $5 bills to anyone coming to visit and told them to move on. A former park manager even said the Statehouse did not make a good museum and that a new museum should be built to house its artifacts in order to return the building to its original purpose as some sort of government office.

While the Statehouse has been maligned and put on the chopping block several times, it has obviously never been closed down.

"When they really think about it, they realize it is a very important part of our history," Camp said of the state legislature's decision to keep the park open.

Hayes concurred.

"I think Territorial Statehouse has such 'staying power' simply because of the amazing story it tells about Utah's struggle to get going," Hayes concluded.

The Huntsman Connection and Revival

Jon M. Huntsman, Jr., who served as Utah's Governor from 2005-2009, has deep roots in Fillmore. His fourth great grand-parents were among its first settlers.

After Huntsman was elected Utah's governor in 2004, knowing that the State Capitol would be under renovation, he decided to deliver his first State of the State address in Fillmore at the Territorial Statehouse to give the oft-forgotten relic another day in the sun. Not only did Huntsman have an affinity for the place because of his family connections, but he also said he wanted to get out among Utahns not living along the Wasatch Front.

In a *Salt Lake Tribune* article three days before the event, Huntsman said that he might be "a little bit unstable" during the speech because of the emotion the town evokes for him.

"My whole family tree is represented in Fillmore," Huntsman said. "It's where I learned how to drive a car, learned how to shoot a gun, fish."

Huntsman's decision to give the speech in Fillmore caused quite a stir. Just as with legislators of old, some members of the state Legislature at the time grumbled at the thought of having to travel one hundred fifty miles for an event usually held in their backyard. Some refused to attend and did end up boycotting the event, saying it was a waste of taxpayer money to stage it so far from the capital.

Event organizers asked Camp to pull portraits of Huntsman ancestors from the museum's hall of portraits in its basement to be put on display during the speech. Camp informed them that there were roughly thirty to forty pictures of Huntsman's forebears on the wall, which would be overkill. In the end, Camp ended up displaying eight portraits—only those with the last name of Huntsman.

Camp said the event, which happened on January 20, 2005, revived interest in the Statehouse, causing a short-lived uptick in visitation. To commemorate Huntsman and to provide visitors with something many of them could relate to, the museum put together a display about Huntsman in one of the rooms on the museum's middle floor.

To build awareness and help generate revenue, nine years ago, Camp set up a program that has turned the park into a venue for historical-themed LDS church youth conferences. The Building Zion Youth Camp has been filling up every slot made available recently. The camps consist of eighty to one hundred youth at a time who camp right on the Statehouse's lawn, which is fitting historically because the first settlers camped kitty-corner across the street on land that became a fort, and the Statehouse's builders camped right next to the building while it was under construction, Camp said.

Just as they were for the early settlers, dances are a staple for the youth groups. In fact, Camp brings in some local youth to help teach the visiting youth the dances. In addition to the youth group dances, the top floor of the building hosts other regular dances throughout the year for locals, including on July 3 to commemorate Independence Day, at the beginning of the school year and a formal dance on January 4—Statehood Day—as well as other times when groups "beg" for one, Camp said.

Camp acts as caller for the dances, but his job isn't like a standard square dance caller. It's a little easier. He says all he does is shout instructions when needed.

The youth camps and the annual Old Capitol Arts and Living History Festival, held annually the weekend after Labor Day, have helped raise awareness of the Statehouse and its history. Camp said actual visitation numbers are hard to calculate if one counts all the people who walk around the building after hours taking pictures, as they often do during the festival.

Camp said just over nine thousand visitors came through the door in 2017, but approximately three thousand enjoyed July 4 festivities, and another six thousand participated in the September festival.

But one thing Camp and most visitors can agree on is the 162-year old building is a gem.

The uneven-floored basement of the Territorial Statehouse
Museum displays many portraits of Fillmore's founders

Fun Historic Stops in Southern Utah

Visiting the Territorial Statehouse

The Territorial Statehouse State Park Museum is located in downtown Fillmore.

Visitors enter from a small addition to the building on the northeast corner. Once inside, the staff will tell visitors to expect uneven floors, especially in the basement, which feels dungeon-esque with all its exposed stone. The basement contains the hall of portraits and the *Deseret News* printing press exhibit, among others. The Huntsman room is on the middle story, whose floors are a little uneven as well.

The building's showcase is easily the top floor (arrived at by a steep set of narrow stairs originating from the room in the southwest corner of the middle floor), the large room where most of the action happened in the building—where the Legislature met and where seemingly innumerable dances and social gatherings occurred.

One cannot help but imagine what it must have been like to see the Legislature at work or attend one of the late-night dances in the room. And to the former legislative chamber's credit, its well-finished wooden floors do not feel uneven.

The original story and photo gallery can be found at the following link:

https://www.stgeorgeutah.com/news/archive/2020/01/26/raw-territorial-statehouse-day-fillmores-ill-fated-mid-19th-century-decision-is-now-a-historic-jewel

FOR FURTHER INFORMATION
Utah Territorial Statehouse State Park Museum website:

https://stateparks.utah.gov/parks/territorial-statehouse/

II.

NORTHERN ARIZONA AND SOUTHERN NEVADA

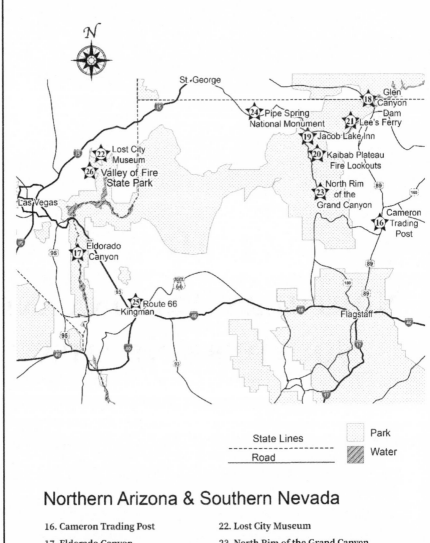

Northern Arizona & Southern Nevada

*The Cameron Trading Post rustic exterior proudly displays
the year of its establishment over a century ago*

16

CAMERON TRADING POST
The Granddaddy of All Way-Stops on the
Way to the Grand Canyon

Along the roadside of U.S. Highway 89 in the high desert plains north of Flagstaff, Arizona, drivers will find numerous stands along the roadside where Navajo artisans sell their wares to passersby. The granddaddy of them all is the Cameron Trading Post.

The Cameron Trading Post is where visitors will find the largest selection of rugs, jewelry, dolls, and practically any Native American art one can imagine. It proudly displays in its windows an insignia noting it's been a fixture on the south side of the Little Colorado River since 1916.

The region now known as Cameron has been a crossroads of trails and roads for centuries. Today its geography is most favorable, serving as the gateway to the South Rim of Grand Canyon National Park. The Grand Canyon, not surprisingly, is on the Top ten list of most-visited national parks in the nation. The trading post, along with its adjacent gallery and hotel, look like they would fit right in a national park given their rustic stone architecture similar to the 1920s style of national park structures, also referred to as parkitecture.

The Early Days

There might not have been a Cameron Trading Post if not for the suspension bridge, built in 1911, which now stands like a museum relic next to the still-bustling tourist center. Back then, the only inhabitants of the area were a few Navajo sheepherders living in hogans in the otherwise barren country.

The one-lane, fourteen-feet wide, six hundred sixty-feet long suspension bridge was the longest one west of the Mississippi River at the time. All materials for the bridge's construction had to be hauled in by wagon from Flagstaff, fifty miles to the south. Names of some of the workmen can still be seen inscribed into the concrete supports underneath the bridge.

The bridge enabled travelers to bypass nearby Tanners Crossing, considered the safest crossing of the Little Colorado River by many groups for centuries, including Native Americans, Spanish explorers, mountain men, government surveyors, Mormon pioneers, and others. The river nearly swallowed wagons and livestock during its regularly-occurring torrential flash floods. The bridge made travel through the area much easier. It was no longer necessary to descend into the Little Colorado's narrow gorge, nearly impassable for much of its length.

Five years after the bridge was built, brothers Hubert and C.D. Richardson claimed 112 acres and built a tin-roof shack on the south side of the river as a trading post. During the first years of business, it served mainly Navajo and Hopi, who bartered their blankets, livestock, and wool for dry goods. At times in the early days, twelve hundred to seventeen hundred head of sheep would be at the post waiting for shipment to Flagstaff or Winslow, Carolyn Davis wrote in her book about the Cameron Trading Post.

In its first iteration, the trading post was a drafty store surrounded by four shacks for accommodations. At the time, a trip to the remote trading post could take days, so the Richardsons housed many customers overnight over the years, treating them like family. The trading post became a way-stop for anyone traveling through Northern Arizona.

The Richardsons also understood local Native American dialects and customs and became vital in ensuring Native Americans understood American legal and social systems.

The post was first known as the Little Colorado Trading Post, but later the name was changed in honor of Arizona Senator Ralph Cameron. Today the name seems an interesting choice since, to his credit, the senator helped develop Grand Canyon into a tourist attraction, but on the other hand, he literally felt he owned part of it—the Bright Angel Trail. He even lodged a legal complaint claiming he was entitled to charge tourists to use the trail even after the Grand Canyon was designated a national park.

During World War I, Davis wrote, the trading post wasn't the only building in Cameron because it was the site of a copper mining camp, which consisted of a huge warehouse and barn.

In the spring of 1928, Hubert Richardson built a pueblo-style hotel out of red stone that was called the Klo-a-chee-kin (Little Red House) Hotel. It included six upstairs rooms for guests as well as a ground-floor lobby, kitchen, dining room, and an apartment for its caretaker.

Once the hotel was built, Cameron became a more popular place and was noted for its luxury in such a remote location. It was decorated with Navajo rugs, baskets, and pottery, and the interior stonework included some stones that included dinosaur tracks. Additionally, there were a couple of hogans for Navajo guests (torn down in the 1930s for easier access to the gas pumps), and the number of cabins for tourists behind the store grew each year. An addition to the hotel, known as the Hopi building, was added in the 1930s.

Cameron became a true oasis in more ways than one. It was the only supplier for miles around of two necessities for automobile travelers—gasoline and tires. It was a welcome respite during the challenge of traversing unpaved roads in sometimes-unreliable transportation.

There have been many additions to the trading post over the

years, including connecting some of the original buildings to form one building, such as the lobby between the actual trading post itself and the hotel guest check-in. Major additions occurred in the 1960s and 1980s, administrative assistant and group manager Bernetta Jensen said, but one thing about all the buildings remained the same: its signature red rock exterior.

They've tried hard to maintain all the buildings over the years, Jensen said, and have recently upgraded many of their rooms.

Brushes With Fame

The trading post lies at the southern boundary of the Navajo Nation. When first established in 1916, it was not part of the Navajo Reservation. The boundary moved several miles to the south in 1934, and in 1940, a special act of Congress deeded the Richardsons the land the trading post sits on, Davis wrote. Because of this, the trading post is an independent business and not subject to Navajo tribal law, she noted.

The business has stayed within the family over the years. C.D. Richardson's grandnephew Joe Atkinson took over the lease in 1977 and formally purchased it in 1983.

Movie stars ranging from John Wayne to Errol Flynn to Humphrey Bogart to Goldie Hawn have stayed at the motel while filming movies in Northern Arizona. Famous Western writers Zane Grey and Tony Hillerman set several scenes in their novels at the trading post. President Richard Nixon was marooned in Cameron during a snowstorm while he was a law student in the 1930s, Davis wrote, also reporting he held secret meetings there while president in the early 1970s.

The Trading Post Today

Just like the Navajo arts and crafts it proudly displays and sells, the history of the Cameron Trading Post is a tapestry of stories of many natives who have contributed to what it is today. Most of its staff is Navajo and Hopi, who, Jensen said, treat each other like family.

While nearby Gray Mountain, just less than ten miles south, is basically dead, Cameron continues to thrive. Jensen said Cameron

*The trading post's gallery displays a variety of
Native American art for sale*

owes its success to the community that surrounds it, a good tourist base, the cultivation of good relationships as well as the exceptional food.

"We try really hard to keep our customers happy" because, Jensen said, customers keep going where they're treated well.

Cameron is one of the last authentic trading posts remaining in the southwest. Today the whole complex boasts a grand gift shop, a restaurant, a sixty-six-room hotel, an RV park, a grocery store, and a gas station. The trading post keeps it in the family as the current manager, Josh Atkinson, is the great-grandnephew of the original founders; and Native American weavers and potters still come to the post to trade.

Tour groups are often booked up to two years in advance, and it is normal to see eight to twelve tour buses in the parking lot. It is a regular stop on the itineraries of many travel companies, Jensen said.

Visitors exploring even for a few minutes will see its allure, not only with its vast displays of Native American handiwork, including its gallery of higher-end wares that was built in 1919. Two of its grand allures are its stonework and the inviting atmosphere of its garden courtyard, originally planted in the 1930s, which forms the centerpiece of its hotel.

"We're an original," Jensen said. "We're not like any other chain."

Visiting the Cameron Trading Post

The Cameron Trading Post is just under fifty miles north of Flagstaff, Arizona, on U.S. Highway 89. It makes a great base camp for visiting other scenic and historical treasures in the area in addition to the Grand Canyon's South Rim, Navajo National Monument, Wupatki National Monument, Sunset Crater National Monument, Lee's Ferry, and Glen Canyon National Recreation Area.

The original story and photo gallery can be found at the following link:

https://www.stgeorgeutah.com/news/archive/2018/06/03/raw-cameron-trading-post-day-this-is-the-granddaddy-of-all-way-stops-when-you-head-to-the-grand-canyon/

FOR FURTHER INFORMATION
Cameron Trading Post website:

https://www.camerontradingpost.com/

Once a rough-and-tumble mining community,
Eldorado Canyon is now home to a variety of obsolete items,
from antique cars to former road signs

17

ELDORADO CANYON
From Lawless Gold Mining Mecca to a Hoarder's Dream

Today, it's part *Twilight Zone* and part Radiator Springs from the Pixar animated blockbuster *Cars*, but a century and a half ago, Eldorado Canyon was the epitome of what one would consider the Wild West.

Visitors driving through this canyon situated about a mile past the town of Nelson on Nevada's State Route 165 cannot help but wonder "How did all of this stuff get here?" as they view the vast expanse of outdated items, from a whole host of antique cars to nostalgic signs that advertise products ranging from soft drinks to motor oil.

The feeling is almost eerie, as items that once had a lot of life in them now stand still, weathered by their complete exposure to the elements—chief among them the scorching Southern Nevada sun.

Taking a closer look, one can find loose resemblances to Lizzie, Doc Hudson, Flo, and Mater of *Cars* fame.

However, there's more of a checkered past than there are checkered flags in the canyon. But the only two items that give an indication of its past upon driving into it are two historical inscriptions on stone installed over fifty years ago. These inscriptions provide a brief snapshot of the canyon's tumultuous gold-mining history, a history that is legendary today.

Gold Fever and Lawlessness

The history of Eldorado Canyon starts with its name, which first appeared in the early 16th century as a Spanish name meaning "the gilded one" and was actually two words—El Dorado.

Americans turned it into a compound word, and "in time, the name came to mean a paradise of riches and abundance," according to Helen S. Carlson's book *Nevada Place Names: A Geographical Dictionary*.

Considering its history, however, the place could hardly be considered a paradise.

Mining in Eldorado Canyon actually predates the mid-19th century, when it was at its height. Before European-Americans arrived, Native Americans extracted turquoise in the area, and Spanish explorers worked what is now known as the Wall Street Mine.

Evidence shows that the Spanish didn't even name the canyon, as one might expect. Instead, it was a steamboat captain making the first foray on such a vessel up the Colorado River in 1857. Captain George Alonzo Johnson wrote about naming the canyon in December of that year, according to the book *Nevada's Turbulent Yesterday: A Study in Ghost Towns* by Don Ashbaugh.

Ashbaugh noted that Johnson's trip opened up the river to steamboat traffic and led to Eldorado becoming the river's busiest port. Steamboats remained a major player in shipping along the river until the early 20th century.

Soldiers camping in the canyon in 1859 struck upon ore samples valuable enough to cause some excitement and staked a claim known as "The Honest Miner," which an uncovering of the canyon's later history reveals is an oxymoron.

Soon after, other claims were laid, some of them with interesting names, including the January, Morning Star, and Techatticup, derived from Paiute words meaning "hungry" and "bread" as Paiutes were reported to have frequented the mining camps begging for food.

This flurry of mining activity led to the development of the Colorado Mining District, named for a remarkable fissure through the rocks carved by the nearby Colorado River. When the mines first opened, they were located in the Arizona Territory. In 1866 they became part of Nevada.

Due to its remote location and lack of machinery, only high-grade, easily-worked ore was extracted, and it was done with picks and shovels by candlelight. By 1863, a 10-stamp, steam-powered mill was set up along the river, and both gold and silver (gold was the main aim, but silver was an important byproduct) were mined. A little bit later, the Techatticup Mine, which accounted for over half the production of the mines in Eldorado Canyon, erected a 15-stamp mill. The bullion was shipped by steamboat down the river to sea-going vessels in the Gulf of California.

By 1865, Eldorado Canyon's population was approximately fifteen hundred, and by that same year, over eight hundred fifty mining deeds had been recorded. Ironically, these early mining operations in the canyon seemed to attract little outside notice, partly due to the area's isolation but also because of overshadowing by larger, more famous mining operations within the state, including the Comstock, Eureka, and Ely mining districts.

The bulk of mining production in Eldorado Canyon took place between 1864 and 1900 and, according to some estimates, produced up to $10 million worth of precious ore, with the Techatticup and Wall Street mines the main producers.

Many of the original miners in the area were Civil War deserters, information that is even chiseled in stone at the site. Deserters came from Army contingents at nearby Fort Mohave and Eldorado.

Later, deserters were described by Ashbaugh as "rough characters seeking a safe place to avoid the dangers of war."

Carlson went on to further describe the scene in her book:

"Filled with both Northerners and Southerners who wished to avoid conscription during the Civil War, it was the scene of claim jumping and murder. Mining law was decided by the 'Winchester's amendment to the Colt statute.'"

But Ashbaugh reported that the shooting at the mines didn't begin until the Civil War was over. According to Ashbaugh's account, the Unionists and the "Rebs" divided into different camps under their respective flags.

"From behind the walls of their stone shelters, they carried on a continuous warfare, albeit mostly verbal," Ashbaugh wrote. "It was about as near as the war ever came to Nevada, although it was several months after Appomattox before the 'battle' of Eldorado came to an end, with no fatalities reported."

There were plenty of fatalities after the war, however.

Stories of the lawlessness of Eldorado Canyon in its early days abound. Fights over gold, women, mining claims, and property ownership sometimes resulted in shootouts. Some greedy miners decided the best way to get what they wanted was to eliminate the competition through murder.

The Techatticup Mine, with quarrels over ownership and management, as well as labor disputes, became the epicenter of the rowdy free-for-all. There were times murder became an almost nightly occurrence. With the nearest lawmen two hundred to three hundred miles away, sheriff's deputies rarely made the trip to keep the peace or investigate wrongdoing.

"I think there never was another place where, in proportion to the population, so many murders were committed without the criminals being brought to trial or even apprehended," wrote Eldorado Canyon gold miner John Riggs in 1880.

A military outpost was established in 1867 to protect steamboat traffic and to keep an eye on local Indians, who were beginning to raid the canyon.

Two Paiute Indians in particular—Ahvote (or Avote) and

Queho—wreaked a lot of havoc, accounting for nearly thirty deaths between them over the course of about twenty-five years from the late 19th century and early 20th century.

Ahvote's demise came at the hands of his own tribe members, who were angry about not receiving handouts from the canyon's white residents because of the ruckus he had caused. They killed Ahvote and took his head in a burlap sack to show that they had truly eliminated the threat.

Queho, responsible for over twenty murders himself, successfully eluded a sheriff's posse after his final murder in 1919. His remains were found in a cave in 1940, identified easily because one of his legs was shorter than the other.

Questioning the Historical Reliability and the Las Vegas Connection

According to several accounts, stories and statistics of the canyon's early history are not very reliable. A 1980 Lake Mead National Recreation Area Historical Study by Mike Belshaw used the words of a G.M. Butler in a 1933 Arizona Bureau of Mines Bulletin that succinctly told why that was.

"The pioneer prospectors and miners were too busy overcoming obstacles, struggling against hardships and celebrating occasional periods of good fortune to write about their experiences, even if able to do so," Butler said. "Few authentic records of most of the earlier camps exist. Available statistics are often far from reliable, and good judgment is required to separate the true from the false."

Belshaw said the early miners "suffered that primitive, age-old, and ineradicable disease"—gold fever.

"One of its manifestations is that ultimately it's not the finding but the search that fascinates," Belshaw explained. "Men have sold obvious bonanzas for pittances to be on their way again."

Many miners were also delusional, Belshaw said, thinking that in the next wash, the next rise, or the next ridge lay a sure-fire, honest-to-goodness "Eldorado." And by the same token, Belshaw noted, miners tended to exaggerate grossly the worth of their findings.

"Next to prospectors, fishermen are paragons of truth," Belshaw concluded.

However, Donna Andress, a native of the area who later wrote a book on its history, told the story of one Techatticup Mine superintendent who actually kept excellent records in the 1880s. One of the funniest things he wrote about was his distaste for a particular brand of margarine that was being sent to the mine, which arrived in a rancid state. Instead of using it for its intended purpose, he wrote about using it to grease the axles of wagon wheels, Andress said.

Interestingly, mining in Eldorado Canyon has a direct connection to the founding of Las Vegas.

One of the pioneers of Las Vegas was a miner-turned-rancher who was first attracted to the area because of its mining interests and did some mining in Eldorado Canyon. Octavius Decatur Gass took over the old Mormon mission and turned it into a fairly successful ranch.

However, he eventually lost it by mortgaging it and some other land to Archibald and Helen Stewart to pay for some litigation in which he was involved, said Michael Green, history professor at UNLV and author of KNPR's segment "Nevada Yesterdays."

Helen Stewart then sold most of it to Senator William Andrews Clark for construction of the railroad, which led to the creation of the Las Vegas townsite.

"So, in a way, it would be reasonable to claim that without Eldorado Canyon attracting O.D. Gass, Las Vegas might have turned out a lot differently," Green said.

Mining in the 20th Century

The coming of the railroad in 1905 revived the mining district with a fifty-ton smelter developed seven miles west of Eldorado Canyon. For closer proximity to the smelter and mines, older settlements were moved to the new town of Nelson (which was incorporated the same year as Las Vegas), where a new cyanide mill was constructed to process the gold.

A 1916 pamphlet touted the canyon's mining as "The New Comstock," but after the turn of the 20th century, the mines didn't produce as much as they did in their more legendary days. When World War II began, the U.S. government shut down the mines so most able-bodied young men of draft age could serve their country fighting the war, Andress said. After the war, a company tried to revive mining by filing for property at the Wall Street Mine location, but once the company found out what it would take to reclaim the land, it gave up. Andress said a few people have mined the tailings in the years since the war and have found some nuggets. Essentially, however, mining in the canyon has ceased.

Ashbaugh corroborated Andress's account, noting that the only mining going on was by a "few Sunday prospectors with modern metal detectors" still seeking gold in "Eldorado's sun-scorched hills."

By the 1950s and 1960s, the main traffic in Eldorado Canyon was made up of those trying to catch "the wily bass of Lake Mohave and the big trout of Black Canyon," Ashbaugh said.

Eldorado Canyon is a popular place for photoshoots
for those wishing to capture nostalgia from the
past among its many obsolete treasures

Modern Day: The Werlys

Tony and Bobbie Werly came to know Eldorado Canyon as they transported canoes back and forth through the canyon for trips that Bobbie Werly guided in the late 1990s. The couple began to think that instead of transporting the canoes back and forth from Boulder City, where they lived at the time, they would inquire about buying property in the canyon to make it their canoeing base camp.

The Werly's daughter, Shauna, said Tony Werly called the owner of the property, whose family had owned it since 1929, to see if he could buy five acres, to which the owner refused. A few months later, the owner called back to say he would sell them all fifty-one acres of property or nothing.

In 1994, two days before the Werlys closed escrow on the property, they found sealed off mine shafts, Shauna Werly said. It was then that the family decided that mine tours would be in the property's future, but they didn't get the tours started until six years later.

When the Werlys bought the property, they also got several mining claims, a store, a stamp mill, a bunkhouse, and a few tin miner cabins, most of them in a dilapidated condition. But since then, more buildings have been brought back that were originally in the canyon.

The people of Nelson had moved the buildings to avoid damage to them, Shauna Werly said, and the old-timers knew which buildings needed to return to the site. For instance, the headquarters of their operation, which doubles as a museum of historical pictures, mining equipment, and other relics, was once the miners' mess hall. All the buildings they've restored have come on their own dime with no grants or contributions from outside organizations.

Old-timers also helped the Werlys find out the history of the place they purchased, along with information gained from a Nevada Historical Society book written by John L. Riggs and published in 1912 entitled *The Reign of Violence in El Dorado Canyon.*

Andress said the Werlys have done well at preserving the area's history and have done a fantastic job at preserving the mine tunnel. Today, the mine tour is the biggest attraction on the Werlys' spread, but there is another draw to the area that Shauna Werly said is made possible by her parents' "hoarding capabilities."

"They've been hoarding for as long as I've been alive," she said.

However, she noted, they never intended on doing what they're doing, which is bringing in a vast array of what some would consider junk in the form of antique vehicles, signs, outdated equipment, and more. It's gotten to the point that the Werlys regularly get calls from people asking if they would take an old vehicle off their hands.

Many people love the nostalgia of the place, Shauna Werly said, and all of the curiosities around have made it popular for photo-shoots—everything from scantily-clad models to family photo sessions.

Shauna Werly said the family never knows who they're going to meet on their property from day to day, but they come from all different walks of life. Lately, she said, there has been an influx of international travelers.

But there is no doubt the Werlys enjoy their gig.

"For me, the history of this place is unreal," Shauna Werly said. "A lot of people can't believe the history."

Visiting Eldorado Canyon

Eldorado Canyon lies just over twenty-five miles south of Boulder City and approximately one mile east of the town of Nelson.

Mine tours are offered at 9 a.m., noon, and 2 p.m. It is best to call ahead to make reservations. Those desiring a photoshoot should also give advance notice and will have to sign a waiver and pay a fee depending on the number in their party.

Visitors to Eldorado Canyon should speak to the Werlys. They love to tell people about the place's history and what they've done with it.

An old bus and mining building grace the eclectic mix of treasures to be found by Eldorado Canyon visitors today

The original story and photo gallery can be found at the following link:

https://www.stgeorgeutah.com/news/
archive/2018/03/25/eldorado-canyon-day-
from-lawless-gold-mining-mecca-to-a-
hoarders-dream/

FOR FURTHER INFORMATION
Eldorado Canyon Mine Tours website:

http://eldoradocanyonminetours.com/
index.html

The Glen Canyon Dam, which created Lake Powell,
has been a controversial engineering marvel since
its construction in the mid-1960s

18

GLEN CANYON
Is the Dam a Tombstone or Giver of New Life?

To some, it's a tombstone.

To others, it has been a giver of new life.

There are few events or issues in the annals of U.S. environmental history that have been as controversial as the construction of the Glen Canyon Dam, what the U.S. Bureau of Reclamation considers a crown jewel and a monument to its success at harnessing the waters of the mighty Colorado River.

To those who opposed the dam, Glen Canyon's history reads like an obituary about the loss of an incomparable sandstone and water wonderland boasting a plethora of Native American ruins, emerald hanging gardens and a few spectacular natural bridges—a place to truly commune with nature and to find complete solitude since few made an effort to traverse the river along the canyon's stretch. Those on the other side of the issue feel the dam has improved Glen Canyon—now providing greater access to its breathtaking contrast of towering crimson sandstone walls and vast expanses of crystal blue water.

No matter what side one is on, the history of the grand red rock spectacle in Southern Utah and Northern Arizona is a compelling one.

Early History

Archaic, Basketmakers, Anasazi, Paiute, and Navajo—those are the names of the Native American civilizations, in chronological order, that have made their homes in the Glen Canyon area.

The first European-Americans to see the canyon were the members of John Wesley Powell's Green and Colorado River expeditions of 1869 and 1871. Powell, the namesake of the enormous reservoir created by the dam, named the now largely-submerged canyon for its hanging gardens and green glens, calling it a "land of beauty and glory." Some say if he were alive today, he would be disgusted that the reservoir that desecrated that glorious landscape bears his name. Through his expeditions down the river on dories, Powell became the patron saint of river rafters, whose adventurous exploits, starting in the 1930s, were the only way to see the vast reaches of Glen Canyon and its tributaries and side canyons.

The Obituary

Glen Canyon wasn't on many people's radar until a dam was slated to be built there.

In the early 1950s, the Bureau of Reclamation proposed the construction of three dams within the Colorado River's upper drainage, one in Glen Canyon and two on the Green River in an area known as Echo Park within the boundaries of Dinosaur National Monument. Echo park particularly raised the ire of environmental groups since it is in the boundaries of a national park area. Such a dam had already been built in a national park, and to environmentalists, that was one too many. In the early

20th century, the Sierra Club fought and lost the fight to stop the damming of the Tuolumne River in Yosemite National Park's Hetch Hetchy Valley, a place club founder John Muir said was as beautiful, if not more beautiful, than Yosemite Valley itself.

Sierra Club Executive Director David Brower, along with a varied cast of contributors, which included famed publisher Alfred Knopf, put together a photo book entitled *This Is Dinosaur: Echo Park Country and Its Magic Rivers*. They gave the book to every member of Congress so lawmakers could see what would be lost if a dam was built. The uproar and propaganda worked as Brower and the Sierra Club successfully made a concession that no dam would be built in Dinosaur or any other national park area. But Glen Canyon neither had such status nor defenders in high enough places. However, it did have defenders.

The earliest proposal by its advocates to grant the area national park status came in 1937, and another came during the deliberations over Echo Park, but both fell on deaf ears and already-made-up minds.

At first, Brower and the Sierra Club felt little remorse in condemning a place to drown that they'd never seen before. But they soon found out that, in this case, ignorance was not bliss. When building the dam became a reality in 1956, they decided to actually go see the canyon for themselves. Once they saw it, they regretted the compromise they had made. As Jared Farmer, history professor at Stony Brook University and author of the book *Glen Canyon Dammed*, explained, Brower realized Echo Park didn't hold a candle to Glen Canyon.

"Beauty is subjective, yet I think it's fair to say that this dam inundated one of the world's most beautiful canyons, not to mention scores of amazing side canyons," Farmer said. "Lamentations about the Glen are largely about the loss of natural beauty. However, many other treasures were lost. The reservoir destroyed tens of thousands of Ancestral Puebloan sites, include-ing rock art panels, apartment complexes, and burial grounds—not to mention various sacred places for Southern Paiutes, Navajos, and other tribal peoples."

The dam also meant the destruction of wildlife, Farmer noted, including "fish, amphibians, birds, mammals, and every other living thing that drew sustenance from a living river."

"In the mid-1960s, when the reservoir first rose, creatures without gills and wings sought refuge on slickrock prominences, which became temporary islands for animal refugees," Farmer said. "In this barren habitat, they fought to the death. Snakes and scorpions lasted the longest, and then they too drowned in the dead pool."

Once Glen Canyon was scheduled for "execution," it became a much more popular place. Many desired to see what would soon be buried in a watery grave. In the late 1950s, archaeologists from the University of Utah started to lead many excursions into the canyon to catalog and gather Ancestral Puebloan artifacts and document the ruins that would be lost in the flooding.

The people most affected, emotionally and economically, were river rafters who had been frequenting the river for years. To the dam's credit, it did make their business brisker from 1956-1962, during dam construction, but to them, it was like spending as much time as they could with a loved one diagnosed with a terminal disease.

Folk singer Katie Lee became a self-proclaimed addict of Glen Canyon based on river runs through it in the 1950s and early 1960s. She even labeled the agency that built the dam, "The Bureau of Wreck-The-Nation." She wrote a tribute to the canyon in a photo book entitled *Glen Canyon: Images of a Lost World* by her river-runner and photographer friend Tad Nichols.

"Glen Canyon was a place where you didn't just see color and shadow; the light acted upon you physically," she said. "It was almost as if some mystical force had you in its beam and moved you about into places you'd never think to go on your own. Where the light didn't send you, the enticing side canyons drew you."

One of the most famous river runners of that time period was Edward Abbey, the famous environmentalist who devoted a whole chapter to Glen Canyon in his bestseller, *Desert Solitaire*.

"I was one of the lucky few who saw Glen Canyon before it was drowned," Abbey wrote. "In fact, I saw only part of it but enough to realize that here was an Eden, a portion of earth's original paradise."

Most river guides did not transition their businesses to the reservoir out of disgust and heartbreak over the dam. The only one who did was Art Greene, who had the foresight to lease formerly barren land that would eventually become Wahweap Marina, where he became the main concessionaire.

In the canyon's waning moments, it served as a stand-in for the Holy Land in an epic movie, *The Greatest Story Ever Told*, a retelling of the life of Jesus Christ.

"How strange it is that a movie that documents the story of the doomed Christ inadvertently documents a doomed canyon," Gary Ladd wrote in the afterword of Nichols' book. "Sometimes, while watching the video, I occasionally push the pause button to stretch a glimpse of some now-drowned landmark or of the living Colorado itself, portrayed in the film as the River Jordan."

Whereas *This is Dinosaur* proved a lifesaver for Echo Park, *The Place No One Knew*, a book of Glen Canyon photographs by color photo pioneer Eliot Porter published in March 1963, essentially became Glen Canyon's obituary, a showcase of a singular landscape no one would likely see again. The book's release date came approximately at the same time the dam's diversion tunnels were closed, which gave birth to Lake Powell.

The Dam Story

Bureau of Reclamation engineers, who had been scoping out an ideal spot to build a dam since 1916, decided on constructing the dam where it is, fifteen miles north of Lee's Ferry due to the canyon's narrowness at the location; the availability of aggregate material nearby to make cement; and canyon walls and a bedrock foundation that were determined to be strong and stable enough to eventually support what would become a 710-foot tall dam.

Congress approved the enabling legislation to build the dam, the Colorado River Storage Project Act, on April 11, 1956, and construction began on October 15, 1956. President Dwight D. Eisenhower pressed a telegraph key from Washington D.C. that set off the first explosion.

Just preparing the site, which included blasting two forty-five-foot wide, three-thousand-foot long diversion tunnels to channel the river's path out of the way of construction and excavating down 137 feet to the canyon's bedrock to construct the dam's foundation, took three and one-half years. Due to the controversy surrounding the dam, part of the construction process for the Bureau of Reclamation was a publicity barrage, Russell Martin reported in his book, *A Story That Stands Like a Dam*. Russell said that Bureau of Reclamation Commissioner Floyd Dominy "was certain that if he got the truth out, if school kids and Kiwanis clubs, Rotarians and Lions and chambers of commerce across the country got the straight stuff about what a boon, what a blessing this dam would be," the criticism would quiet down.

To aid in public relations, the bureau produced a film entitled *Canyon Conquest* in 1959 in which an old Navajo man is the central character and inspects the bridge and dam construction site to understand it and to "pronounce it good," Martin wrote. By the end of the film, even though the dam was still a mystery to the man, "the narrator offered the assurance that at least he knew it would mean 'energy-pulsing, flashing power . . . life for the swarming population as yet unborn,'" of course referring to the electricity the dam's turbines would produce.

Several important things were built prior to the dam before construction could even commence: roads and electrical lines to the remote area, a company town to house workers (Page, named for former Bureau of Reclamation Commissioner John C. Page), and a bridge so that construction workers wouldn't have to take a two-hundred-mile trip just to get to the other side of the river.

The roads built connected to form U.S. Highway 89. Page was established in 1957 and incorporated in 1975. The bridge, whose central arch towers six hundred eighty feet above the river, was the highest bridge in the world at the time it was finished in 1959. Each of these three integral precursors ended the area's isolation.

That isolation was one of the challenges of the dam's construction—getting the necessary materials and equipment to the site. Trucks came from Kanab, Utah, and Flagstaff, Arizona, around the clock with fresh supplies.

Construction on the actual dam itself did not begin until June 1960, when concrete placement began. Concrete was poured using twenty-four-ton capacity buckets by way of an aerial tramway strung across the canyon from a concrete batch plant protruding out of the side of the canyon. Additionally, as concrete was poured, workers had to install cooling pipes that carried water from the ice plant to cool the concrete to help it cure during the hottest months.

Constructing the dam was a dangerous proposition. One of the most dangerous jobs was that of the men known as "highscalers," who descended down the face of the canyon walls to prepare it for construction, including inserting bolts and mesh to prevent rock-falls. They later descended down the dam to complete tasks such as tightening bolts.

Dan Barlow, of Santa Clara, had another dangerous job working on the dam. He was a carpenter who put the concrete forms up.

"My specific job was to loosen the bolts on the forms after they had been poured and cured," he said. "To do so, I had to climb over the form on the outside, take a big ratchet gun and remove some of the bolts while loosening others so the lifter could just take them right off."

Sometimes the danger of the job would scare Barlow.

"I would go on the outside of the forms, lean on my belt and look down in between my legs and I would see the ground six hundred feet below me!" he said. "I stayed doing that clear to the top and out on the face of the dam."

Barlow said he witnessed a man fall through an elevator shaft 135 feet to his death. With a total of approximately two thousand workers during dam construction, there were only eighteen deaths, and those came without the more rigorous safety protocols that would be in effect today.

Barlow had a simple philosophy to keep himself safe.

"I just learned to . . . make sure I was hooked to something solid," he said. "That's the whole secret to staying alive—tie yourself to something that counted."

"Glen Canyon Dam emerged from bedrock incrementally, as a series of blocks seven and a half feet high and up to sixty feet wide and two hundred ten feet long," the Bureau of Reclamation's history page about the dam noted. "Work on constructing the dam continued twenty-four hours a day until on September 13, 1963, the last of over four hundred thousand buckets of concrete was placed."

Impoundment began forming the reservoir in March of that year, approximately six months before the dam's actual completion, and the reservoir did not reach full capacity until June 1980.

An interpretive panel at the dam's visitor center touts the needs the dam met, saying:

"Glen Canyon Dam serves as the final storage that allows the Upper (Colorado River) Basin to deliver the required water to the Lower Basin. It also regulates river flow, controls flooding, stores water for human use, including irrigation, and generates electricity. Its reservoir, Lake Powell, has become a world-famous recreation destination."

The old turbine on display on the deck of the Glen Canyon Dam is a reminder of its purpose in addition to water storage—hydroelectricity generation

A New Life?

One of the mandates of the National Park Service mission is to provide enjoyment for visitors, and many would argue that Lake Powell, part of Glen Canyon National Recreation Area, has done just that. However, it hasn't done it in the way the original proponents for making the Glen Canyon area a national park envisioned. Regardless of its national park status, Lake Powell has definitely made Glen Canyon a recreation mecca accessible to the average tourist. Anyone with access to a watercraft can explore its vastness, including picturesque side canyons.

Early Lake Powell boosters foresaw it as the hub of what they called the "Golden Circle," a cluster of scenic attractions including Grand Canyon and Zion national parks.

"New beauties revealed by the modern lake approach are worth the sacrifice of former rugged primitiveness," Arizona Highways' editors noted on the lead page of an article written about the lake soon after its birth.

In the early days of Lake Powell, Farmer reported that visitors wanted to visit Page and its surroundings because of its "rugged primitiveness," almost feeling as if they were pioneers in the "Wild West."

"At first, nothing save water and slickrock existed between Wahweap and Hite, a distance of almost one hundred fifty miles," Farmer wrote. "Boaters had to carry their own gas and plenty of it. Waterskiing wasn't allowed. There were no patrols at first, no buoys marking the maze of side channels."

Farmer noted that even the Park Service acknowledged its primitiveness, admonishing visitors to "be carefree but not careless," and saying: "This is a place for recreation, but it is just emerging from its wild state."

Today, Lake Powell has emerged from that wild state and is dotted with marinas and other tourist accommodations and developments across its 186-mile length (when full). For Utahns especially, Lake Powell is practically a rite of passage—a regular vacation destination. It has become the top houseboating lake in the nation, and with its extremely long channel, water-skiers can go for as long as they can stand.

"Many families and large groups enjoy houseboat trips for reunions and exploring side canyons by kayak or small boat, with hiking in formerly very remote areas," said Glen Canyon National Recreation Area archivist Cindy Stafford.

To Stafford, Lake Powell is "a lake that stretches one hundred forty miles even when half full with nearly two thousand miles of geologic wondrous shoreline to explore," as well as "a photographer's dream (and) also inspiration for many other artists and writers."

Fishing is also a big draw at Lake Powell, which hosts annual tournaments, she also noted.

The dam has had an effect on wildlife, both positive and negative. John Spence, chief scientist for Glen Canyon National Recreation Area, said the dam negatively affected the native fish.

"They were already in decline due to the presence of exotic fish such as channel catfish, brown trout, and carp," he said. "Current efforts are underway to restore the native fish, and there has been recent significant success with these efforts in the upper portions of Lake Powell."

The dam has helped the resurgence of other fish populations.

"The Colorado River below the dam changed from a muddy fluctuating river to a clear cold system benefitting rainbow trout," Spence wrote. "The sixteen mile stretch of Glen Canyon that remains has a highly successful trout fishery."

There has also been a resurgence of waterfowl such as ducks, gulls, terns, waders, and shorebirds since the birth of Lake Powell, Spence noted.

Is there a balance to be found in Glen Canyon and Lake Powell? Without them, much fewer people would venture to see the area's superb scenery. Without them, the town of Page might not even exist. Without them, the area would not be as economically robust; for example, the national recreation area accounts for approximately 3,419 local jobs, a recent federal report noted, and spending in local communities by park visitors exceeded $240 million in 2016.

But with the dam and the lake, there are still those who lament what could still exist if the canyon had not been inundated and who feel that Lake Powell isn't living up to its primary purpose: water storage. There are still calls to drain the lake, chief among them from the Glen Canyon Institute, an advocacy organization whose goal is to restore the Colorado in Glen Canyon to its free-flowing former glory. The Institute's position is that a fuller Lake Mead would lead to less water loss via evaporation and seepage through porous sandstone than it would having two separate reservoirs.

"The Bureau of Reclamation is initiating a three-year study on Lake Powell to better quantify evaporation rates, starting this spring," Spence explained. "This study will inform decisions made by the Bureau of Reclamation regarding lake levels for Lake Powell and Lake Mead."

Some on the anti-dam side say that the dam cannot stand forever. In fact, Rebecca Solnit, in a recent article entitled "Letter From a Drowned Canyon" in *The California Sunday Magazine*, wrote that she sees evidence that the drop of Lake Powell's water, specifically where the Dirty Devil River meets the lake, has caused the river to carve its channel deeper, lusher vegetation to appear on the banks of silt, and natural processes that have started to restore the river to how it used to look.

"'Nature bats last' was a favorite motto of the radical environmentalists of the 1980s, but what 'nature' means now that human beings have altered the climate itself is hard to say," Solnit wrote. "What's not hard to say is that Lake Powell is dying, and from its corpse, the Colorado River is emerging."

What one must consider when looking at the history of Glen Canyon is that much of the literature available—and there is plenty—leans toward the dam-detractor side. Those have the loudest voice, it seems, but cannot be considered the majority.

In fact, Spence wrote that he does not recall speaking to anyone who bemoans the dam's existence during his entire National Park Service career.

"Page is a pretty quiet town, and not a lot of discussion goes on here about the issue that I have heard," he admitted.

Of course, there are many who would lament Lake Powell's death, were it to die as Solnit perceives. All those who enjoy its recreation opportunities from year to year would certainly view its death as a major travesty.

Visiting Glen Canyon Dam/Lake Powell

Glen Canyon Dam and its Carl Hayden Visitor Center are located adjacent to Page, Arizona.

Tours of the dam originating from the visitor center are offered daily. More information on tours is available on the Glen Canyon Dam's tours web page.

Lake Powell itself offers a variety of recreation opportunities emanating from its several marinas which are, from south to north, the following: Wahweap, Dangling Rope, Hall's Crossing and Bullfrog.

The original story and photo gallery can be found at the following link:

https://www.stgeorgeutah.com/news/archive/2018/02/25/raw-glen-canyon-day-is-the-dam-a-tombstone-or-a-giver-of-new-life/

FOR FURTHER INFORMATION
Glen Canyon National Recreation Area website

https://www.nps.gov/glca/index.htm

The rustic exterior of the Jacob Lake Inn, gateway to the North Rim of the Grand Canyon, has not changed much over the years

19

JACOB LAKE INN
A Rustic Getaway En Route to the North Rim

The story goes that some visitors to Jacob Lake Inn burst through the door in their swimsuits, goggles, and floaties ready for a water recreation experience and are disappointed when they find out there really isn't much of a lake and what purports to be the lake is approximately a mile away from the actual inn itself.

Some refer to it as "the lake that ain't," while the website for Kaibab Camper Village, near where the lake is actually located, refers to it as "a pretty little pond in a horse pasture."

Named for Mormon pioneer leader Jacob Hamblin, Jacob Lake in Northern Arizona was once an important source of water because there is practically no freestanding water on the Ponderosa-pine-covered Kaibab Plateau.

The inn's story started in 1923 when Harold and Nina Bowman, of Kanab, saw tourist potential in the area and established a makeshift service station, selling gas from a fifty-gallon barrel in the back of a truck.

"If we could sell a barrel of gas in one day, we thought we had had good business," Harold Bowman later recalled of that first year.

A year after starting the service station, the Bowmans established a lodge. It was rudimentary at first, just a two-room cabin with quilts for doors. Only fifty years before Jacob Lake Inn's founding, that same road had been a Paiute migrational trail, later expanded into a wagon road by Hamblin and other Mormon settlers who were shown the route by the Kaibab Band of Paiutes.

The product of Mormon pioneer stock themselves, the Bowmans went into the venture undaunted. They even raised their two young children, Effie Dean, born the same year they set up shop, and Harold Jr., born in 1927, while operating the enterprise, and the children began working at a young age. Effie Dean started emptying slop jars in the rooms at age seven, while Harold Jr. started taking firewood to all the cabins at age four. They washed dishes, cleaned rooms, emptied slop jars, gathered firewood, and moved on to other jobs. Eventually, Harold Jr. and his family became involved in other interests and left the business, but Effie Dean continued strong, even after her marriage to John Rich Sr. It is her children who own and operate the inn today.

Jacob Lake Inn's first location, established in 1923, was nearer the lake, but in 1929 it was moved closer to the road at the junction of U.S. 89A and State Route 67, which leads motorists to the Grand Canyon's North Rim. After the construction of the new road, Harold Bowman felt the highway junction's position at the base of a large hill would be inconvenient and more challenging for travelers headed to the Grand Canyon; so he borrowed a grader from the Forest Service and graded what he felt was a better road, making the junction on flatter land right in front of Jacob Lake Inn.

The government road was "not exactly ideal for vehicles whose primitive brakes and underpowered motors needed a lot of space to make a run up the slope, or to slow down for that matter," said

Melinda Rich, part of the fourth generation of Jacob Lake Inn's founding family.

Lucky for Bowman, what he graded became the official road when it was paved in the mid-1930s.

In the first few decades of the inn's establishment, it was still the "Old West" in the area, Effie Dean's son John Rich Jr. said. He and his siblings own Jacob Lake Inn today. To illustrate his point, John Rich Jr. recounted a story of two of his great-uncles chasing two bandits who tried to rob the inn's gas station in the winter of 1933. They notified the sheriff so he could set up a roadblock and chase the robbers down the mountain. When they saw the road-block, the bandits ran off into the desert; but the sheriff built a fire near it, telling the great-uncles the two would soon be back. Sure enough, the bandits eventually returned and surrendered.

In an era when large corporations usually buy up such businesses, Jacob Lake Inn bucks the trend. It holds the longest-standing Forest Service permit in the nation issued to the same family, John Rich Jr. said. Some permits are older, he noted, but in those cases, ownership has changed. The inn is truly a family business; of John Rich Jr.'s twenty-nine nieces and nephews, all of them have been employed at Jacob Lake Inn at one time or another.

The inn has been a family affair in other ways as well.

"We have at times employed grandchildren of former employees," John Rich Jr. said. "We always have children of former employees."

Additionally, there have been many occasions when the inn's employees have met future spouses through their work there.

"Everyone is friends at Jacob Lake," Melinda Rich said. "We work to help people learn to live and work together. That can be challenging with each new set of employees, but it is worth the atmosphere it creates in the lodge on and off work."

To Melinda Rich, Jacob Lake is the very core of her existence. She said:

> *Jacob Lake and working with my extended family is the foundation of my sense of self. I spent every summer at Jacob Lake until I was 26. I learned from*

my grandparents, parents, aunts and uncles and cousins how to cook, to lead, to be enthusiastic, to plan parties, to sing, to be generous and welcoming to people I've never met; to drive, to love beauty in nature and in people, to see the consequences of people's actions, to see the hand of God in my life, to be adventurous and funny."

Vanda Wadsworth worked at Jacob Lake Inn during the summer of 1959 just after graduating from high school. Jacob Lake Inn was a very friendly atmosphere in which to work, she said. During their time off, employees had a lot of fun, some of which was provided by their employer. One of the most exciting things she recalled employees doing in their free time that summer was coasting on bikes down U.S. 89A East toward Houserock Valley and Lee's Ferry . . . without having to pedal back up since a truck was waiting at the bottom to take them back uphill. Effie Dean also organized trips to the Hopi Reservation for employees to watch snake dances.

Another favorite activity during Wadsworth's time at the inn was walking bikes up the hill south along Route 67, climbing the Jacob Lake fire lookout tower, and then coasting back down on bikes. Watching Kaibab squirrels, indigenous only to the Kaibab Plateau, jump from tree to tree was also memorable for her. "It was like watching the monkeys in '(*The*) *Jungle Book*,'" she said.

Effie Dean was always very nice to her employees, Wadsworth said. On a return trip to Jacob Lake, Wadsworth happened to run into Effie Dean a few years before she died in 2013. The matriarch of Jacob Lake remembered her face but not her name, Wadsworth said, and they had a good chat.

After a more recent return trip, Wadsworth said she felt like not much has changed at the lodge since she worked there, especially to its exterior.

Jacob Lake Inn Today

The lodge's main building purposely has a rustic feel, John Rich Jr. said. The inn's oldest accommodations are cabins built in the 1930s. The latest addition is a twenty-four-room motel building constructed in 2005. In total, Jacob Lake Inn has sixty-two rooms.

May, June, September, and October are the busiest months at Jacob Lake. Surprisingly, July and August are slower because potential visitors think it's too hot in Arizona in the summer.

The busyness of the winter traffic depends on the weather; more people come if there is snow to cross-country ski and snow-mobile.

"Winter snowmobiling is spectacular," John Rich Jr. said. There are Forest Service roads on many ridges ideal for the snow "machines," and some of those roads offer different viewpoints of the Grand Canyon.

He remembers that Reece Stein, outdoor reporter for Salt Lake City's KUTV, came in the winter of 1972-73 and did a feature on snowmobiling the Kaibab Plateau, complete with images of a snow-dusted North Rim. The report caused somewhat of a sensation, John Rich Jr. said, and Jacob Lake Inn was booked nearly solid the next winter with excited snowmobile enthusiasts. Trouble was, he said, it didn't even snow that winter.

It does snow most years, he said, and when it does, "the snowmobiling is as good as it gets." For example, Rich said a snowmobile club from Flagstaff has even made the Kaibab Plateau its home base.

Other than being a friendly stopover on the way to the North Rim of Grand Canyon National Park, Jacob Lake Inn is also known for its "home cooking."

In 2009, Arizona Highways made a list of the one hundred best things in Arizona and listed Jacob Lake Inn cookies as one of them. Buzzfeed once said one dessert that readers needed to eat before they die is the inn's "Cookie on a Cloud," which landed at number eleven on its list of twenty-six treats from around the world.

"We bake most of our own bread, and all of our entrees are made from scratch," John Rich Jr. said. "We have no frozen entrees."

The gift shop at Jacob Lake Inn is a showcase of Native American arts, and crafts and John Rich Jr. gives presentations there about Navajo culture on Tuesdays, Thursdays, and Saturdays. Mondays, Wednesdays, and Fridays, his brother Matt Rich offers a photography program.

Historically, inns have been proprietors' homes guests were invited into. Jacob Lake Inn is just such a family business in the truest sense of the word. It is a place people can come and relax, John Rich Jr. said.

"We're in the recreation business," he said. "We have purposely stayed away from modern conveniences."

The inn's rooms are rustic—especially the cabins that date from the 1930s—and don't include TVs "so people can get away from it all."

On occasion, they do get complaints from guests, but at the time of this writing, the inn currently boasts an eighty-nine percent approval rating on TripAdvisor.

"Any family business has its complications and squabbles and drama," Melinda Rich said, "but what I love most about my family is that we can always come together in love, find solutions, forgive, and find a better way."

Visiting Jacob Lake

Jacob Lake is only a half-hour drive southeast of Fredonia, Arizona, on U.S. 89A. It sits only forty-four miles north of the North Rim of the Grand Canyon, which is the end destination of most travelers passing through.

Even if one is not staying at Jacob Lake Inn, it is worth the stop to peruse the gift shop or have a bite to eat and enjoy its charm. Next door, a Kaibab Plateau Forest Service Visitor Center provides visitors information on other activities in the area, including climbing one of the Plateau's fire lookout towers to learn about the service's fire management and enjoy stellar views.

Jacob Lake isn't the only lodging choice in the area. A Forest Service campground is just across the highway, the Kaibab Camper Village is less than a mile south, and Kaibab Lodge is twenty-six miles south.

*Jacob Lake Inn's cabins do not offer some modern amenities
that some guests might expect because they are
designed to truly get away from it all*

Author's note: Vanda Wadsworth, who is quoted in this story,
is the author's mother.

*The original story and photo gallery can be found at the
following link*:

https://www.stgeorgeutah.com/news/
archive/2019/06/02/raw-jacob-lake-day-a-
rustic-getaway-en-route-to-the-north-rim/

FOR FURTHER INFORMATION
Jacob Lake Inn website

https://www.jacoblake.com/

The Jacob Lake lookout tower, just south of Jacob Lake Inn, is the Kaibab Plateau lookout tower that receives the most visitors

20

KAIBAB PLATEAU FIRE LOOKOUTS
Modern-day Rapunzels in a Job Almost Obsolete

There are a few modern-day Rapunzels on the Kaibab Plateau, but they don't have to let down their hair in order for anyone to access their lofty perches. There are stairs to climb for those who want to pay them a visit (if fear of heights isn't a problem). They welcome visitors because it breaks up what can turn into a monotonous day, and they enjoy sharing what they do, which is central to the U.S. Forest Service's mission there.

The lookout towers are holdovers from a program started over a century ago that is being phased out in other states but has staying power in this isolated forest in Northern Arizona, partly because of the area's topography. Most lookout towers are built on high mountains, but the Kaibab towers are on a plateau and don't have that luxury, so they were built above the tops of the trees to provide needed vantage points.

The Forest Service's fire lookout program started in 1905, originally as platforms in tall trees with boards fastened to the trees as ladders. The agency started building wooden towers in the 1920s, and in the 1930s, the metal ones sprang up.

The Jacob Lake and Big Springs towers, both one-hundred-foot Aermotor MC-39 models, were built in 1934 by contractors from Kanab, Utah. The Dry Park Tower was built in 1944, an Aermotor MC-99 model that is one hundred twenty feet tall. The enclosed platform at the top of the towers is seven feet by seven feet, and a cabin was built at the bottom of each tower as residences for each lookout.

"Because of the topography, they're still very valuable," Connie Reid, North Kaibab Ranger District archaeologist and tribal liaison said, explaining that those who man the lookouts do an excellent job at spotting smoke.

The Kaibab National Forest does still utilize aircraft to monitor the forest, but usually, after storms and in places out of the towers' range, she said.

"Fire lookouts don't have the limitations that aircraft sometimes do," North Kaibab Ranger District Public Information Officer David Hercher said. "For example, fire lookouts can be staffed earlier and for longer periods of time. They are less likely to be impacted by inclement weather and reduce the risk of exposure to pilots."

Those manning the lookout towers work five days a week. Their hours can be extended when fire danger is extreme or when a fire is going on to watch fire behavior because it can be erratic in the wind. When the fire danger is at its highest, they can work ten-hour days and sometimes six days a week. Lookouts work seasonally, usually from May to October.

Surprisingly, this hasn't been a job with high turnover over the years. One lookout has been climbing the towers for over twenty years, and Big Springs Tower lookout Ross Rogers has been spending summers on the Kaibab Plateau off and on since 1949 when he was a child. His father, Royce Rogers, who was a fifth-grade teacher in the Phoenix area, took a summer job as a lookout in the Dry Park Tower that year and his parents kept coming back year after year. It helped that his mother, Mavis Rogers, was originally from nearby Moccasin, Arizona.

"They just loved it," Rogers said of his parents' summer job. "It was almost like we were going on a camping vacation for the summer."

The family stayed in a cabin near the tower, but it truly was just a step above camping—a one-room cabin to which the Forest Service added a lean-to extra bedroom to accommodate the eventual seven children the Rogers added to their brood. There was no electricity and no running water in the cabin, which was only equipped with a wood-burning stove. They had to carry water in a ten-gallon bucket from a cistern in a nearby meadow, they used Coleman lanterns for light, and his mother did laundry by washboard.

One of Rogers's most memorable moments from those summers spent on the Plateau was being drug across the meadow, holding onto a rope with a calf at the end of it. He said he also remembered the excitement of when his parents would see smoke, and the children just had to climb the tower to see it for themselves. The tower became the children's monkey bars, and they'd also play a game in which they'd drop a rock from the top to see if it could reach the bottom without hitting any part of the tower. Usually, the rocks didn't make it much past halfway without hitting a part of the tower. And they did all of this with no guardrails on the stairs like there are now, Ross said.

In the late 1960s, the Rogers family moved from Dry Park to the Big Springs Tower, and even after his father died in the 1970s, his mother kept up the work until 1999, when she was nearly eighty. As things turned out, she encouraged her son to apply for the job, and he became her replacement. He had just retired from following in his father's footsteps in another realm, teaching fifth grade in the Las Vegas area. In 2000, he followed both of his parents' footsteps, climbed back up the tower, and has been there every summer since. He was happy for the chance to move back to Moccasin to help his mother in her waning years. She died in 2011.

Kaibab National Forest and Grand Canyon North Rim Interagency Fuels Specialist Dave Robinson said the forest has been fortunate to have lookouts like Rogers who have been there a long time and bring with them a lot of institutional knowledge as well as a great pulse on the lay of the land, which leads to better effectiveness. It takes a unique person to be a lookout, he said, and that morale among the lookouts has been good from year to year because they have a special connection to the forest, none more so than Rogers.

"They are a very important part of our team," Robinson said.

Climbing to the top of the Jacob Lake Fire Lookout Tower gives visitors a view of the Kaibab Plateau 80 feet above the ground

A Typical Day in the Tower

The fire lookouts check-in at 8 a.m. and get readings on the weather that they relay back to the dispatch office in Williams,

Arizona. Readings include visibility, wind speed, humidity, and temperature.

The lookouts stagger their lunches, so there is always a lookout in at least one of the towers. After lunch, lookouts weigh "fuel sticks" to measure fuel moisture. It is important to track fuel moisture because they can aid fire management in predicting fire behavior firefighters may encounter when responding to a wildfire, Robinson said; the lower the fuel moisture, the more active the fire behavior may be.

They give another weather report to dispatch at lunchtime as well. Weather reports consist of numbers that equate to certain weather patterns, such as the number two, which means half cloudy to the number nine, which means storm with lightning, Rogers said.

With so much downtime in the tower, Rogers said he reads a lot and listens to the radio, but sometimes he just likes to turn off the radio, listen to the birds and enjoy the peace of the forest. To pass the time, he said his mother made doilies and Christmas ornaments she gave to others as gifts.

"We really enjoy visitors," Rogers said. "It breaks up the day."

When visitors come, Rogers said he explains how the firefinder works, what he does, and why it's important. He also points out the scenery visible from his tower, which includes the Grand Canyon in Arizona, parts of Zion and Bryce Canyon national parks, and the Pine Valley Mountains in Utah, a little bit of Kanab, Utah, and Fredonia, Arizona.

Even with great visibility, Rogers said he can't see the other towers because of the ridges in the way but said he has flashed a mirror from the tower, and his wife could see it from Moccasin, Arizona.

The lookouts are an important part of the Forest Service's interpretation and education, Robinson said.

"Due to the remoteness of most of the district, reliable communications can be a challenge as cell phones will not work in most locations," Hercher said. "For this reason, fire lookouts also serve as vital communications links for emergency services throughout the district."

Robinson received only three hundred visitors all summer last season due to his tower's more isolated, less accessible location. In fact, his mother was quoted in a book about fire lookouts saying that, if she had visitors, they were usually lost. The Jacob Lake Tower, which sits right by the main highway, received approximately thirteen hundred visitors last summer, Robinson said.

Rogers said his wife has gotten used to his long absences as a fire lookout. He stays at the cabin near the lookout during the week and comes home on weekends, but he said sometimes he receives visitors that stay more than a few minutes—family members who stay with him for a time in the summer. For instance, a ten-year-old granddaughter came and stayed a week with him during the summer of 2017.

Lightning and Wind

Lightning is the main perpetrator when it comes to fires, and lightning strikes seem to beat the odds in the towers because, as Rogers explained it, they almost invite lightning to hit them.

Since 2000, Rogers said his tower has been hit by lightning five times while he's been sitting in it.

"It's grounded really well," Rogers said of the tower's ability to absorb lightning. "I don't really worry about it anymore. It's all over before you even know it."

The lookouts sit on stools with glass legs to further help insulate them from lightning strikes.

The tower swaying in the wind hardly fazes Rogers anymore either.

"You get used to it," he said of the wind.

Lightning strikes and having to climb the tower in seventy-mph winds have been Rogers' most exciting moments on the job, he said.

Another memorable moment Rogers related was when a little boy got scared and ran down the tower during a storm. He reached the bottom of the tower just before lightning struck it, Rogers recounted. If the boy would have been on the tower when the lightning struck it, he could have died.

Where There's smoke . . .

Spotting smoke is, of course, the main reason the lookouts are up there.

When the lookout sees smoke, he or she uses a device called the Osborne Firefinder, which helps the lookout determine the direction of smoke once spotted by providing a directional bearing, called an azimuth.

"The lookouts use that angular distance from their fixed position to estimate the distance, which is challenging on the Kaibab Plateau because there are no peaks to use as reference points," Hercher said.

Today, the lookouts can call each other or dispatch to help estimate distances and get a cross-reading from each tower, but when Rogers was a child, they didn't have that luxury.

"Most of the time, we see the smoke," Rogers said. "We usually don't see flames."

Lookouts also must pay attention to the color of the smoke, which gives an indication of what's burning. For instance, burning dead and down fuels like needles typically produce white smoke. Tree torching typically produces black smoke, Hercher said, and blue smoke can typically indicate burning vegetation like shrubs.

The smoke's location, its color, its size, and whether it is growing are the four main things lookouts tell dispatch when they see it, and they continue to monitor the smoke for crews on the ground until the crews arrive on the scene.

Robinson said it is important to monitor the smoke because, in some cases, it might not be smoke at all. Sometimes it can be residual water vapor or fog during the monsoon season.

Most fires on the Kaibab Plateau are caused by lightning, about ninety percent, while humans cause only approximately ten percent of them, Robinsonsaid. One year, Rogers said, there were eight fires going at the same time during one lightning storm. Sometimes the Forest Service simply lets fires burn to help restore the ecosystem, depending on the place and time.

"A vast majority are single trees that we suppress," he said of those fires.

The towers are still a valuable resource, Rogers said, vital in spotting and monitoring fires.

"Sometimes we pick them up before the planes even get in the air," he said.

The ascent to the top of a Kaibab Plateau fire lookout tower should not be attempted by those fearful of heights

Visiting the Kaibab Plateau Fire Lookouts

A visit to the fire lookouts on the Kaibab Plateau should start at Jacob Lake, Arizona, located just under thirty miles southeast of Fredonia, Arizona, on U.S. Highway 89A.

The most accessible fire lookout is the Jacob Lake Tower, located on the left (east) side of the highway just over a mile south of Jacob Lake Inn on Arizona State Route 67 (the Grand Canyon

Highway). A visit to a fire lookout would be a nice addition to a trip exploring the Grand Canyon's North Rim.

For information on visiting the other lookouts, Big Springs and Dry Park, drop by the Forest Service's Kaibab Plateau Visitor Center just south of Jacob Lake Inn. The Visitor Center can provide directions and/or maps to the other lookouts.

At heights of one hundred and one hundred twenty feet above ground level, climbing up to the top of the lookouts might not be ideal for those with a fear of heights, but the stairs are enclosed by railings, giving a certain measure of security.

Those who climb the towers will be rewarded with expansive views and an interesting conversation with the Forest Service's first line of defense in fire management.

The original story and photo gallery can be found at the following link:

https://www.stgeorgeutah.com/news/
archive/2017/08/13/dsr-raw-fire-lookout-
day-modern-day-rapunzels-on-the-kaibab-
plateau/

FOR FURTHER INFORMATION
Forest Fire Lookout Association website:

http://www.firelookout.org/index.html

*"Lee's Fort" was the original building constructed on the site of
Lee's Ferry; it served as both living quarters and office*

21

LEE'S FERRY
An Important Pioneer River Crossing,
Failed Mining Location and River Rafting Hub

On a winter day, Lee's Ferry in Arizona is a serene place—a
showcase of a wide, slowly flowing river contrasted by surrounding
towering red rock cliffs. Only a few visitors walk along the trail
near the riverbank, taking in its majestic scenery.

This peaceful setting belies the bustling activity at this picturesque former river crossing during warmer months as well as the
important role it played in history—the linchpin of the Mormon
pioneer migration into the Arizona colonies.

The main reason for its significance over the course of its
history is because it is the only place along the river for seven
hundred miles with direct, easy access to the riverbank by land.

Lee's Ferry, also identified as Lees Ferry, is also a geologic division point, basically where Glen Canyon ends and the Grand Canyon begins. It serves as an important point for the United States Geological Survey and Bureau of Reclamation to gauge streamflow between the upper and lower basins of the Colorado River in order to determine water allotments for members of the Colorado River Compact.

Today it is best known for being ground zero for anyone taking a Grand Canyon river trip.

Earliest History

The first human inhabitants in the Lee's Ferry vicinity were the Ancestral Puebloans, whose ruins in the area date back to approximately 1125 A.D. Later, Paiutes roamed the area and interacted with Franciscan friars Silvestre Velez de Escalante and Francisco Dominguez, who were the first Europeans to view the future Lee's Ferry in October 1776.

Jacob Hamblin, Mormon trailblazer and missionary to the Indians, was the next white man to see the area, crossing the river near the future ferry for the first time in 1858. Hamblin participated in the first successful crossing of the river by ferry while on a mission to warn Navajos to stop raiding Utah settlers at what was then known as Pahreah Crossing in March 1864, building a raft sturdy enough to carry fifteen men, their supplies and horses.

Hamblin realized that the future ferry site could be the doorway to Mormon expansion into Eastern Arizona and encouraged Mormon church president Brigham Young to establish a permanent crossing to aid those potential pioneers. Young chose John D. Lee for the job, and Lee gladly accepted, thinking it would be a great place to evade authorities seeking his capture for his role in the 1857 Mountain Meadows Massacre.

Lee, along with his wives Emma Batchelor and Rachel Woolsey, moved to the ferry and started to eke out a living on what became known as the Lonely Dell Ranch, named for Emma's first reaction at seeing the place.

Lee launched the first ferryboat, appropriately named the "Colorado," in January 1873, and the period of 1873-1875 proved a busy one for the migration into Mormon Arizona colonies along the Little Colorado and Salt rivers. Another busy period came just after construction of the St. George temple of The Church of Jesus Christ of Latter-day Saints was finished in 1877, prompting many couples from the southern colonies to make the trek north to solemnize their marriages in the temple on what became known as the "Honeymoon Trail."

The church built what became known as Lee's Fort in 1874, and it still stands today. The building served as a home, trading post, and school for ferry operators' families.

After being on the run from authorities for seventeen years, Lee was captured in 1874 and eventually executed in 1877 for helping perpetrate the blackest chapter of Mormon history.

The Trying Life of Ferryman Warren Johnson

Howard Spencer, the bishop of Long Valley, where Glendale, Orderville and Mt. Carmel lie, was tasked with choosing Lee's successor as ferryman, finding prospects among those who were opposed to the United Order, the Mormon concept of communal living, and found his man in Warren Johnson of Glendale. Johnson, however, was an unqualified volunteer, having no experience previously in the duties he would be assigned as ferryman. One thing he had going for him was that he and his family hit it off well with Emma Lee, which helped him and his two wives, Permelia and Samantha, be successful and smoothed the transition.

In taking a page out of Hamblin's book, Johnson became adept at getting along with the Navajos that would frequent the ferry, learning that laughing and joking with them while trading would get the job done, earning him the nickname Ba Hazhoona, or "Happy Man," P.T. Reilly reported in his book, *Lee's Ferry: From Mormon Crossing to National Park*.

Johnson learned the river's nuances in a hurry and became the go-to expert on river crossings.

When the river's water was high and powerful, Johnson only dared to take a more manageable skiff across the river, which necessitated taking wagons apart to fit on the smaller boat, leading to grumbling among many passing travelers.

On one occasion, May 24, 1876, a party led by Daniel H. Wells, counselor to Brigham Young in the First Presidency of the LDS church, wanted to cross the river as soon as possible to return to Salt Lake City after visiting the Arizona settlements, but Johnson warned against such a crossing on the regular ferryboat in such turbulent water and recommended taking the safer but much more time-consuming method of dismantling the wagons and putting them into the skiff. Impatient, Wells demanded that they cross in short order and they succeeded without incident in their first two crossings, but the third crossing proved disastrous when the party lost control of the boat in the river's wrath, losing a few wagons and provisions and, more importantly, the life of Bishop Lorenzo Roundy.

Due to the dangers of venturing into the river in torrent stage on long, ungainly ferryboats with higher capacities, Johnson continually tried to convince the First Presidency to allow him to build an easier-to-manage, one-wagon capacity ferry, but to no avail. One time, they spurned his advice and "awarded" him with a forty-seven-foot longboat.

"Johnson knew, when he saw the plan, that God had not inspired the brethren who designed it, but he said nothing and resolved to do his best," Reilly wrote of this instance.

No one knows exactly if Johnson got approval from higher authorities or took it upon himself, but in the winter of 1886-87, he built his own one-wagon ferryboat.

At times, Johnson was doing the work of three men, having to tend the ferry and make a subsistence living from the farm. Some travelers ended up paying their ferriage through work, which was welcome to Johnson. In fact, he built small shacks with the express purpose of serving as accommodations for those laying over at the ferry. He convinced his brother-in-law, David Brinkerhoff, to be his partner at the ferry for approximately five years. During that period, Brinkerhoff was in charge of the farm, so Johnson could devote most of his time to his ferry duties.

For a time, the ferry had two sets of ferry rates—the missionary rate, for Mormon immigrants, and the rate for "other travel." For instance, in 1879, the missionary rate for a wagon and single team was $2, while for other travelers, it was $3. A little later, however, all travelers were given the same rate.

One aspect of paying ferriage continued to haunt Johnson during his stay as ferryman. Some travelers paid their ferriage in perishable goods, which had to be consumed immediately by the ferryman's family, leading to a debt to the church for the amount the perishables were worth. Johnson feared the brethren would eventually require him to pay this debt and wrote letters to Salt Lake seeking his status on the matter, letters whose replies did not address the issue or misunderstood it. Eventually, these debts were forgiven at the close of his service as ferryman.

The incident that shook Johnson and his family's faith the most during their time at the ferry was the deaths of four of the Johnson children to diphtheria contracted from passing travelers in the spring of 1891.

"What have we done that the Lord has left us, and what can we do to regain his favor again?" Johnson wrote in a heartfelt letter to then church President Wilford Woodruff on July 19, 1891.

Woodruff and his two counselors replied that Johnson had done no wrong, that the Lord loved him, and they likened his troubles to the trials of Job, Reilly reported in his book.

Another trial, indirectly started by Woodruff and church leadership, would eventually help lead Johnson away from the ferry. The manifesto ending the church's practice of polygamy in 1890 caused great reflection in Johnson. Before the manifesto, federal authorities spared him from being prosecuted for practicing polygamy, but knowing now that it was church doctrine, he could not give up one of his two wives and their families. He left the ferry in 1896. His first thought was to flee all the way to Canada, but he eventually settled in Wyoming, where he lived the final years of his life paralyzed after he broke his spine in a wagon accident. He died on March 10, 1902.

Gold Mining in Red Rock?

Just as silver was discovered in sandstone at Silver Reef in the 1860s, flecks of gold were discovered in the sands and gravel bars near the river banks in the vicinity of the ferry in the late 1800s.

During the 1880s and 1890s, quite a bit of prospecting took place in the area.

"Some gold was found, but few, if any, struck it rich," authors W.L. Rusho and C. Gregory Crampton noted in their book *Lee's Ferry: Desert River Crossing.*

"Most prospectors soon discovered that expenses almost always exceeded income," they wrote.

Two overly optimistic prospectors who had visions of striking it rich were Robert B. Stanton and Charles H. Spencer.

In 1899, Stanton built a mile-and-a-half road along the south riverbank above the ferry and, in 1900, installed a dredge to extract gold farther up the river near where Bullfrog Marina is now. By 1901, Stanton abandoned his operation.

Spencer came with his American Placer Corporation in 1910 and set up operations at Lee's Ferry. He hoped to use high-pressure hoses utilizing water pumped from the river to sluice the gold from the Chinle shale, sending that sluiced material by flume to an amalgamator set up to attempt to remove the gold. He even built a steamboat, dubbed the "Charles H. Spencer," to transport coal along the river as fuel for his equipment.

Spencer's steamboat became a microcosm illustrating his false optimism and failure. The craft, designed for much tamer rivers like the Sacramento, was not very successful in navigating the more powerful Colorado and was eventually beached and never operated again, succumbing to the unforgiving river over the years. So too, Spencer's operation terminated by 1913.

The Ferry in the 20th Century

By the early 1900s, traffic at Lee's Ferry had become practically a trickle, mostly locals. With the emergence of train travel, even though trips covered more miles, they took less time, which was preferable.

The LDS church sold its interest in the ferry to the Grand Canyon Cattle Company in 1909 and Coconino County, Arizona, took it over in 1910 (its first ferrymen under county ownership were Warren Johnson's sons), operating it until June 7, 1928, when its worst-ever accident killed three men, including Warren

*The remains of Charles Spencer's boiler still
greet visitors of Lee's Ferry today*

Johnson's grandson Adolph, closing it for good. Even before the accident, similar past incidents had already become the impetus to start construction on a bridge in 1927.

From June 1928 to January 1929, when the bridge opened, highway travelers could not cross the river at any point between Moab and below the Grand Canyon. This, however, caused headaches for the bridge contractors as they had to send trucks on an eight-hundred-mile trip to cross the river at Needles, California, to arrive at a destination only eight hundred feet from the starting point, authors W.L. Rusho and C. Gregory Crampton noted in their book. The original Navajo Bridge was replaced in 1995 with a wider one that could better accommodate today's traffic. The historic bridge is now a pedestrian bridge offering sweeping views of the gorge below and the surrounding landscape.

Starting in the 1930s and 1940s, the main purpose of Lee's Ferry shifted to recreation, with river rafters and sport fishermen becoming its main clientele. Its place as a water recreation mecca was cemented in 1972 when it became part of Glen Canyon National Recreation Area.

Today a typical morning at Lee's Ferry between April and October features a crowded boat ramp with boaters and rafters and their guides readying themselves for an adventure on the river.

Two bridges, built sixty-six years apart,
stand together along U.S. 89A near Lee's Ferry

Visiting Lee's Ferry

Lee's Ferry is 46.8 miles east of Jacob Lake in northern Arizona on U.S. Highway 89A. Along the route, drivers pass through dramatic changes in scenery, from the forested Kaibab Plateau to the somewhat barren but picturesque House Rock Valley.

Before reaching Lee's Ferry, visitors should stop at the Navajo Bridge Interpretive Center, open seasonally between March and October. The displays, markers and interpretive signs at the interpretive center will whet the visitor's appetite for the history and scenery to come with visits to Lonely Dell Ranch and the ferry itself. Visitors should be sure to venture onto the historic Navajo Bridge for sweeping views of the river below and the towering Vermilion Cliffs surrounding the spot.

Before reaching Lee's Ferry, a stroll to Lonely Dell Ranch will give visitors a sense as to what life was like for the families of ferrymen with its cabins and outbuildings, orchard and cemetery. At Lee's Ferry itself, visitors can walk along the Lee's Ferry Trail to view the area's intact buildings from different eras, including Lee's Fort, Spencer's American Placer Corporation offices and buildings used by the USGS. Along the trail, hikers can also see a boiler used by Spencer's operation, the top of his steamboat peeking out of the water near the riverbank, as well as an old cable used in later ferry operations.

Visitors hoping to enjoy a Grand Canyon rafting trip or guided fishing excursion should make reservations well in advance before they plan to come.

The original story and photo gallery can be found at the following link:

https://www.stgeorgeutah.com/news/
archive/2019/12/29/lees-ferry-day-all-
about-the-important-pioneer-river-
crossing-failed-mining-location-and-river-
rafting-hub/

FOR FURTHER INFORMATION
Glen Canyon National Recreation Area Lee's Ferry web page:

https://www.nps.gov/glca/planyourvisit/
lees-ferry.htm

*A replica of an Ancestral Puebloan dwelling like
the ones found at the "Lost City" is on display
at the south end of the Lost City Museum*

22

LOST CITY MUSEUM
The Continuing Search for Clues About Ancestral
Puebloan Life in Southern Nevada

Anyone who knows U.S. history well knows that media and advertisements in the 1920s tended to sensationalize reality.

That was certainly true of the moniker given to Nevada's "Lost City" during that time period, which was originally known as Pueblo Grande of Nevada by the archaeological team that excavated it in the mid-to-late 1920s. The more sensational name of Lost City is the one that has stuck.

However, today that name might not seem quite as sensational. Pueblo Grande is essentially "lost." The waters of Lake Mead cover most of it. The information gleaned from the initial excavations was also "lost" to researchers for quite some time. And finally, its museum is "lost" to many travelers who frequent Southern Nevada.

Lost City Museum Director Mary Beth Timm admits that most of the museum's visitors "discover" the museum by chance while driving along Nevada State Route 169, otherwise known as Moapa Valley Boulevard, through Overton. Timm said such visitors are delighted to find such an archaeological gem, with an actual archaeological site inside the museum itself and another one on the north side of the museum grounds, as well as replicas of others on the south side. But unfortunately, visitors aren't able to see the grandest of the ruins, which were the inspiration for the museum because much of it is underwater.

Discovery and Early Excavation

There had been references to Puebloan ruins in Southern Nevada since the late 19th century, but it wasn't until the early 20th century that the reports were confirmed.

James Scrugham, Nevada's governor from 1923-1927, asked locals to be on the lookout for Native American remains. Brothers Fay and John Perkins from Overton recognized broken pieces of pottery and the outlines of ancient structures along the barren ridges near the confluence of the Muddy and Virgin rivers and the town of St. Thomas, which was originally settled by members of The Church of Jesus Christ of Latter-day Saints and was also flooded after the construction of the Hoover Dam.

The Perkins brothers reported the existence of the ruins to Scrugham in 1924, and excavations by a team of archaeologists from the Museum of the American Indian and the Heye Foundation (which was later absorbed by the Smithsonian) led by Mark Harrington began in November of that year after Scrugham's insistence.

Scrugham became the driving force for the excavations, hoping to attract more tourists to the area, and his efforts led to national and international attention pointed toward the discovery. Scrugham even personally arranged site visits for newspaper and magazine writers, who were often given pieces of pottery and arrowhead fragments as souvenirs, according to an article in the

Summer 2010 issue of *The Journal of Southwestern Anthropology and History*.

To capitalize on the fame, a Lost City Pageant was held in May 1925, complete with a constructed replica of an Ancestral Puebloan dwelling. Misinformation about Pueblo Grande, unfortunately, was widespread. Some of the most prominent exaggerations were that Pueblo Grande was the largest city in the Western Hemisphere in its heyday as well as the oldest city in the world. Another was that it was inhabited by seven-foot giants, which Harrington debunked in his writings about the excavation.

This was the start of near-constant archaeological work occurring in the area until 1941, completed with the help of the Southwest Museum of the American Indian and the Civilian Conservation Corps. Work was halted because of two major factors, the filling of Lake Mead and the start of World War II, which obviously directed resources and national interest away from archaeology.

Previous to the discovery, archaeologists thought that the Ancestral Puebloan people were concentrated in the Four Corners area, but Pueblo Grande proved that they thrived much farther west, becoming the westernmost discovery of the ancient people. The ruins provided valuable insights into how the Ancestral Puebloan people lived.

Harrington wrote an article about his findings, which appeared in the July 1925 issue of *Scientific American*.

Harrington made it a point to mention that Native Americans were part of the big dig. "It seems truly fitting that Indians should take part in the expedition of this sort, especially when Indians can be found who will take such a personal interest in the work and will give such careful and intelligent service," Harrington said.

The excavation found numerous houses ranging from structures with only one or two rooms to more "pretentious" buildings, according to Harrington's account, that contained twenty-one rooms. The dig offered a solid snapshot of what life was like for these ancient people.

Residents of Pueblo Grande and the surrounding area "gathered wild natural products of the desert, such as mesquite beans and screw beans," Harrington noted. They also farmed the valley lowlands, growing crops such as beans, corn, and squash. The early Latter-day Saint settlers found old irrigation ditches as they cleared the land, evidence that the ancient peoples irrigated their crops.

For meat, the Ancestral Puebloans hunted deer and other game and raised no domestic animals except for dogs, Harrington wrote. Apparently, the people who lived in the Pueblo Grande were excellent weavers. Harrington reported that his team succeeded in saving a few crumbling bits of fine woven cloth, which reveal that cotton could have been part of Ancestral Puebloans' agricultural products (or was obtained through trade) and that they had also mastered the skill of dyeing textiles.

"Some of the pieces, in texture like cheese-cloth, still showed traces of color, red and blue and purple," Harrington wrote.

These ancient peoples even weaved furs, as shown by evidence uncovered by Harrington's team. The ancient people cut the furry skins of rabbits and other animals into long, narrow strips that were twisted and woven into blankets. They also used feathers to make cloth, which Harrington reported must have been a laborious process.

"It was necessary first of all to gather and prepare fiber, then twist it into strings, and then to wrap these strings with downy feathers until a soft, fluffy yarn was produced," Harrington wrote. "Then came the less tedious labor of weaving this yarn into a blanket."

These people also produced jewelry such as pendants of turquoise, selenite, and shells, which almost certainly came from the Pacific Ocean, revealing that they engaged in intertribal trade. Their arrow-points, drills, and knives demonstrate they had nearly perfected the art of chipping stone, in Harrington's opinion.

The archaeological team found pottery in abundance during the dig, much of which was plain black pottery. However, they also found more ornate pieces, including "bowls and jars of white, and gray and rich red color on which tasteful designs had been drawn with black paint," as well as "pottery in which the decoration was worked out by—varied corrugations of the outside surface."

The most primitive of the dwellings Harrington and his team found were oval pits dug down into the earth to a depth of two to three feet, measuring eight to ten feet in length, while the later dwellings were rectangular and partitioned into separate rooms. Harrington said in his article that the houses excavated date about to the time of Christ, but that the exact time might never be known.

The one break in archaeological work in the area was from 1931 to 1933 on account of the Great Depression. But work started up in 1934 with the Civilian Conservation Corps taking the lead with one company doing excavation and infrastructure work and one company building the museum. Fittingly, one of the last companies of men working on excavation to save the artifacts from being lost underneath the future Lake Mead was Fay Perkins, one of the men who originally reported the ruins' discovery.

Those 1920s and 1930s excavators thought that Pueblo Grande would be underwater in perpetuity, but some of it has reemerged as Lake Mead has dropped. In fact, Timm noted that the whole town of St. Thomas was once completely underwater but has now reemerged, and interpretive panels were recently placed there with the anticipation that the town's ruins would not be under-water again.

There have been excavations since then, but not quite to the same scale as the ones completed in the 1920s and 1930s, Timm said.

The early 20th century digs were the largest excavations ever undertaken in Southern Nevada, and large-scale excavations aren't funded that much anymore, Timm explained. Without that archaeological work, she said, the Lost City could truly have been lost forever.

More Recent Excavations

Those early 20th century excavations have been the main source of information about the Lost City, but many Southwestern archaeologists have been unaware of their legacy, as reflected by the absence of Southern Nevada from many archaeological maps of the Southwest, Karen Harry and James Watson reported. Harry is a professor of anthropology at UNLV, and Watson is an anthropology professor at the University of Arizona as well as a curator at the Arizona State Museum. Both have been part of the most recent fieldwork.

The two authors note that early fieldwork was done by a multiplicity of organizations, leading to many of the materials collected and field notes written becoming scattered over the years. Another reason the early fieldwork is relatively unknown is the lack of a book on the findings, which was a major regret of Harrington, the two authors wrote.

Additionally, "because the Lost City excavations spanned the early half of the twentieth century, much of the data we would recover today was not collected," Harry and Watson explained. "In 2005, archaeologists from Lake Mead National Recreation Area and the University of Nevada Las Vegas set out to remedy some of these shortcomings."

This archaeological team completed excavations of "House 20" in what is known as the "Main Ridge community" to glean more information. One of the earlier excavations' weaknesses was they were majorly concerned with searching and finding museum-quality pieces and overlooked more mundane items such as ground stone items, pottery shards, or chipped stone debris.

For instance, one of the findings of the 2006 fieldwork could be considered more mundane but revealed an interesting tidbit about Ancestral Puebloan life.

"The abundance of ash pits, burned bone, and midden deposits recovered during our excavations indicate that cooking regularly took place outdoors at this location," Harry and Watson wrote.

One of the overarching conclusions with the new data collected was that "the inhabitants of House 20 were heavily invested in agriculture and utilized wild resources that could be obtained in the immediate vicinity," they wrote.

Three of those "wild resources" included bighorn sheep, mule deer, and rabbits. The two authors concluded that rabbits, being most abundant and easily caught, were a major source of food, and that evidence indicates the Puebloans trapped cottontail and hunted jackrabbits in the surrounding desert. Sometimes these rabbits, as well as other small rodents, were easy prey because they were attracted to the Puebloans agricultural fields and engaged in what Harry and Watson termed "garden hunting."

One of the major points of evidence supporting the early inhabitants' dependence on agriculture is the large quantity of storage space in their dwellings, which, through macrobotanical analysis, showed to contain corn. The high proportions of cob fragments suggest that the Puebloans used corn cobs for fuel, Harry and Watson explained.

But even though the 2006 excavation added interesting information for a better overall picture of daily Ancestral Puebloan life, Harry and Watson cautioned readers that the insights were only from one site and only represent one time period. More investigation will be necessary to understand how these ancient people lived during different time periods and in different locations.

The Museum

The Civilian Conservation Corps built the original museum as well as the replica Pueblo houses on the foundations of actual ruins in the mid-1930s. The CCC constructed the museum to resemble a Pueblo dwelling, with a later wing constructed to cover an authentic pit house.

Originally, it was called the Boulder Dam Park Museum but later changed to Lost City Museum to conform to the more popular and accepted name.

"We are the only state museum actually on top of ruins," Timm said.

The museum's displays show visitors a timeline of Puebloan chronology and provide a snapshot of what these forebears of today's Native American tribes faced to survive.

When the National Park Service turned operation of the museum over to the State of Nevada in 1952, it took everything that was on display. The State turned to private collections for artifacts for exhibits and purchased the items in 1973, Timm said.

About a third of the original artifacts found during the early excavations have been in a repository in Reno, but in 2017 they were moved to a repository in the Las Vegas area, she explained. None of those items are on display yet.

Regardless of what specifically is on display, the museum provides a fascinating snapshot of the region's ancient inhabitants. Its displays include pottery, baskets, and arrowheads, as well as other artifacts utilized by the Ancestral Puebloans.

A trip to the Lost City Museum would make an ideal companion visit to Valley of Fire State Park and the ruins of the St. Thomas ghost town.

The original story and photo gallery can be found at the following link:

https://www.stgeorgeutah.com/news/archive/2018/12/16/raw-lost-city-day-the-continuing-search-for-clues-about-ancestral-puebloan-life-in-southern-nevada/

FOR FURTHER INFORMATION
Lost City Museum website

https://www.lostcitymuseum.org/

Grand Canyon Lodge, built in a style known as "parkitecture," was built using locally sourced materials so it would blend into its surroundings

23

NORTH RIM OF THE GRAND CANYON
Dendroglyphs, Deer Herds and the
Golden Age of Tourist Development

It's one of the seven wonders of the world and a UNESCO world heritage site.

One mile at its deepest from rim to river, the Grand Canyon is a literal open book of the layers of geologic history. Some say it was carved over eons of time by the Colorado River and other erosive forces, while others say its formation took less time, a result of a catastrophic event such as an enormous earthquake.

No matter to which formation theory one subscribes, anyone can agree that the Grand Canyon is a breathtaking scenic spectacle, everyone from the first Native Americans who inhabited the area to John Wesley Powell, the famed river explorer who named it, to the six million tourists on average who annually visit it today.

Most visitors flocking to see the Grand Canyon go to the more developed South Rim and skip its northern counterpart. If visitors could travel as the crow flies, it would only be a ten-mile journey from the South Rim to the North Rim. Instead, it is a four-hour, 213-mile drive over a mostly two-lane highway.

When it comes to history, the South Rim is also more well-known. However, the North Rim has its own interesting story.

The Grand Canyon Grazing Kingdom

Settlers of the Church of Jesus Christ of Latter-day Saints started running cattle and other livestock on the Kaibab Plateau near the North Rim as a summer range in the early 1870s. According to an essay by Amy Horn, entitled "Stories Among the Aspen: Running Cattle on the North Rim and North Kaibab" found in a compilation book called *Reflections of Grand Canyon Historians* edited by Todd Berger, by the late 1880s, there were as many as two hundred thousand sheep and twenty thousand cattle on the Kaibab Plateau. One of the early cattle companies on the plateau was the Kaibab Land and Cattle Company, organized by John W. Young, a son of Brigham Young, the second president of the Church of Jesus Christ. The United Order of Orderville had quite a significant herd there as well. By 1907, however, the Grand Canyon Cattle Company had bought out the smaller companies' interests and became the conglomerate of all early cattle operations, Horn wrote.

During the late 19th and early 20th centuries, the Grand Canyon changed statuses in the eyes of the Federal Government. In 1893, President Benjamin Harrison's administration set it aside as the Grand Canyon Forest Reserve, then in 1906, it became the Grand Canyon Game Preserve. National monument status followed in 1908, and in 1919, Congress designated it Grand Canyon National Park, as it is known today.

As the levels of government protection increased, so did the limits on grazing. For instance, in 1916, the Grand Canyon Cattle Company had a permit for fifteen thousand head of cattle, but that was significantly reduced the following year to two thousand. National Park Service managers allowed grazing at first, but gradually phased it out. By 1924 grazing within the North Rim's boundaries had ceased. Even after it was phased out, however, cattle wandered in until the Civilian Conservation Corps built a boundary fence in 1941.

Reminders of these early cattle operations abound on the Kaibab Plateau in the form of aspen dendroglyphs, which are names and dates carved into the aspen's white bark. Archaeologists have recorded nearly five hundred aspen dendroglyphs on the North Rim, which date from the 1890s to the 1950s, but most of them were carved in the 1910s and 1920s, Horn reported. These tree carvings usually occurred near water sources and along trails and, in addition to names and dates, sometimes included cattle brands or even a poem.

Many might consider these dendroglyphs mere graffiti, but Horn noted in her writings that they provide significant insight into these early cattlemen. One such insight that at first puzzled archaeologists was the fact that many of the dendroglyphs along the Point Imperial Trail show dates in December and January when the area, at approximately eight thousand feet in elevation, is usually blanketed with a significant amount of snow, Horn wrote.

A tale from an old-timer solved the mystery. It explained that cattle were driven from the Kaibab Plateau down to House Rock Valley to the east in the fall.

"Cowboys would return to 'ride the points' in December after the heavy snow forced the strays to the canyon rim," Horn explained. "It is easy to picture cowboys riding through the snow, searching for strays, and pausing to record their wintry visit."

"If you look closely among the trees, you can find the stories left by these pioneers," Horn concluded.

The Kaibab Deer Crisis

In the 1920s and early 1930s, Grand Canyon park managers learned a valuable lesson about wildlife management: Don't eliminate predators. At the time, deer on the Kaibab Plateau were protected to the point of persecuting and almost eliminating mountain lions and other predators, J. Donald Hughes wrote in his book *The Story of Man at the Grand Canyon*.

Without this significant predator, the deer population increased rapidly, from an estimated four thousand in 1906 to about one hundred thousand by 1924, Hughes wrote.

"The vegetation suffered as the deer browsed it to the point of disappearance," Hughes explained. "A 'high-line' appeared in the trees as the deer ate every green thing they could reach, and the forest took on the appearance of a carefully clipped city park."

As a result, in the winter of 1924-1925, thousands of deer died of starvation, but predators were still being blamed.

Some other steps besides introducing predators were taken to try to remedy the problem, including relocating the deer.

In 1924, a Flagstaff man was given permission to drive from three thousand to eight thousand deer from the North Rim to the South Rim on the Nankoweap and Tanner trails. During this forced migration, "a line of 125 men was formed on the North Rim to drive the deer to the head of the trail," Hughes recounted.

Those men, armed with noisemakers, moved forward.

"A storm broke, some lost their way, and when they reached the chosen point, all the deer were behind them," Hughes wrote. "Another attempt was not made."

Some fawns were captured and taken to other areas to start new herds. For instance, some of the fawns were flown across to the South Rim, but grew up to be quite tame and became a nuisance. Other fawn transplants were even less successful, with many of them dying in transit.

By 1924, deer hunting on the Kaibab Plateau began in limited numbers, but not within the boundaries of the park. The shooting of predatory animals still continued until 1931, after which the NPS realized it needed to restore the balance of nature by allowing predators into the park.

North Rim Tourist Development: The Utah Parks Company

Up until the 1920s, the North Rim's services for tourists were more rustic, almost by design, as administrators felt such services fit the less frequented area, Michael F. Anderson wrote in the park's administrative history, entitled, *Polishing the Jewel.*

Grand Canyon Lodge stands today as an excellent
example of "parkitecture," the construction of
national park facilities using locally-sourced material
designed to blend in with its surroundings

Some of those first who tapped the tourist potential in the area were Kanab residents Edwin "Uncle Dee" Woolley and his son-in-law, David Rust, who, starting in 1907, offered outfitting services from Kanab, just over eighty miles away from the North Rim, but discontinued their venture by 1919. In that same year, "Uncle" Jimmy Owens left his job as a Forest Service game warden to offer hunting trips within the Kaibab National Forest, grazing a buffalo herd along the plateau. However, records show that the buffalo preferred to graze in House Rock Valley than in the park itself, Horn wrote.

Arizona Strip residents Aldus "Blondie" Jensen and his wife, Melissa, offered saddle trips along the rim and down Bright Angel Creek. Brothers Chauncey and Gronway Parry, automobile dealers based in Cedar City, Utah, who would later be the driving forces behind Kanab's fame as a significant western moviemaking locale, also got into the act by including the North Rim in their public transportation network that transported visitors to Southwestern Utah's parks and monuments.

According to Anderson, Elizabeth Wylie McKee operated the principal North Rim concessionaire at Bright Angel Point from 1917 until 1927.

"Her father, William Wallace Wylie, had pioneered the 'Wylie Way' concept of park concessions at Yellowstone in the 1880s, which consisted of a camp with a central dining room and primitive lodge flanked by individual tent cabins," Anderson wrote.

Wylie himself started the camp at the Union Pacific Railroad's request and entrusted the North Rim facility to his daughter, who acquired ownership when her father retired in 1924. She managed the camp with the help of her son, Bobby, and a small staff of local teens while her husband, Thomas, guided trips to Point Sublime and Cape Royal.

The 1920s was the decade that saw the most development along the North Rim, some of which survives to this day. In 1925, the National Park Service built a ranger cabin, warehouse, barn, and machine shed at Bright Angel Point. Duplex cottages, along with a few outbuildings and a developed campground, followed in 1926. For a decade, the McKees used to haul water via burro or mule from springs just below the rim within Transept Canyon.

One of the burros they used for this job was nicknamed "Brighty." Bobby befriended the abandoned burro, and the two worked well together in the grueling job. Bobby 'paid' Brighty for his work by giving him a stack of "flapjacks." The formerly wild burro endeared himself to visiting children, allowing them to ride him. Marguerite Henry's children's book, *Brighty of the Grand Canyon*, immortalized the mule, and a statue of him sits prominently in the Grand Canyon Lodge. Many believe that rubbing the statue's nose will bring them good luck.

In 1927, however, the park eliminated the need for this chore by building a system that would pump twenty-four gallons of water per minute from those same springs to a storage tank to serve the growing development in the area. Despite the fact that fewer than ten thousand visitors annually visited the North Rim at the time, the development of these state-of-the-art water and power systems, a half-million-dollar project, represented a remarkable investment, Anderson noted.

"Aside from these investments, the Utah Parks Company extended water, sewer, and electrical lines to its developed areas and supplied most utilities to NPS administrative buildings free of charge," Anderson wrote.

In 1927, the Utah Parks Company (UPC), a subsidiary of the Union Pacific Railroad, became the major concessionaire for the North Rim. Unfortunately, this meant the end for those who had been previously operating concessions at the North Rim. They were forced to sell to the UPC. However, the McKees completed the 1927 season, and the Parrys and Jensens were able to operate a few more years while the UPC built its lodge.

Built in 1927 to 1928, Grand Canyon Lodge honed in on the same village concept as Zion Lodge, with one hundred standard cabins and twenty deluxe cabins surrounding the main lodge. The complex also included employee quarters, postal and telegraph services, and visitor entertainments. Part of that entertainment provided from the young UPC staffers became singing to visitors as they arrived and "sing-aways" as they departed.

The famed architect Gilbert Stanley Underwood, who was also responsible for the lodges at Bryce Canyon and Zion, designed the lodge to blend in with its natural surroundings using locally-sourced materials in its construction. This concept became known as "parkitecture."

A fire destroyed the original Grand Canyon Lodge and two of its deluxe cabins in 1932. The main lodge was rebuilt in 1936-37, utilizing much of what remained of the stone foundation, piers, walls, and chimneys of the original building. The rebuild retained the general configuration of the first lodge with a few exceptions. The UPC added fifteen-bedroom men's and women's dormitories the same year the new lodge was finished. Some say the recreation is not as architecturally spectacular as the original but retains its "Underwood flavor" even though it is not clear if he was part of the reconstruction. Grand Canyon Lodge takes full advantage of its location on the rim, boasting a viewing room with large windows within the lodge itself, a viewing deck on its east side, and a dining room that overlooks the rim as well.

Before the 1930s, transportation to and from the North Rim was a difficult proposition as most of the roads in the area were simply leftovers from early settlers and freighting efforts. The Forest Service improved the route from Jacob Lake to the North Rim, which was "pretentiously dubbed the Grand Canyon Highway," Anderson wrote, even though it was far from the quality of today's highways.

In fact, those roads were "in such poor condition that during the early 1920s the tiny towns of Fredonia and Kanab supported half a dozen service stations, whose employees spent much of their time combing the Arizona Strip for stranded motorists," Anderson noted.

Construction on a new access road to the North Rim began in 1927 and closely followed the path of an old wagon road worn by cattlemen and, interestingly, improved by the Bureau of Entomology, Anderson noted. It included a 2.9-mile spur to Point Imperial (formerly known as Skidoo Point) that followed earlier wagon tracks.

"The difficult, serpentine road was completed by three separate California contractors in 1931 at a cost of well over half a million dollars," Anderson wrote.

One reason the UPC did not hesitate to make such ground-breaking improvements was the promise of that North Entrance Road but also the knowledge that state road agencies planned to construct highways throughout Northern Arizona and Southern Utah that would make easier connections to it.

Not surprisingly, during World War II, the Utah Parks Company curtailed services at the North Rim, and visitor numbers declined significantly. In 1948, the UPC signed a twenty-year concessionaire contract with the park service as visitation returned and then exceeded prewar levels.

"In the ten years following, the National Park Service allowed the company to write off more of its park-related expenses, but the short travel season, high costs, fixed rates, and economy-minded tourists would guarantee losses for another quarter-century," Anderson wrote. "Despite a new contract and return to the prewar trend of escalating visitation, the Union Pacific Railroad held back on major tourism-related investments."

The company was reluctant to make costly improvements because it had seen only an average of seventy percent occupancy rate for its lodging facilities since 1950. Demand exceeded supply only a few days a year, and the company knew it had to achieve profitability, not believing the National Park Service's optimistic visitor number projections. As such, it resisted the NPS's demands to improve its facilities during the Mission 66 program, which aimed to improve and build new facilities to commemorate the Park Service's 50th anniversary.

When the contract expired in 1968, the Union Pacific Railroad wanted to get out of the tourist industry and sell the UPC. It had a deal on the table, but it fell through in 1969. It only completed annual contracts from then on, and in 1971, it donated all of its facilities to the NPS and ceased operations. In 1972, the NPS opened up a bidding process for a concessionaire and TW Recreation Services, a subsidiary of Trans World Airlines (TWA) got the contract, ending what many would consider the golden age of tourism at the North Rim, as well as the Utah Parks Company's other holdings in Zion, Bryce Canyon, and Cedar Breaks.

Today's visitors will still enjoy these rustic accommodations and have a clear picture of what it looked like back then as little has changed since these structures' initial construction.

Visiting the North Rim

Unlike the South Rim, the North Rim is not open year-round. It operates approximately May 15 to October 15, sometimes closing later, depending on snowfall.

The main tourist area of the North Rim is centered around the Grand Canyon Lodge and the Bright Angel Point Trail. It is home to the North Rim Visitor Center and many other visitor services, including eateries, gift shops, and a campground.

Visitors will be rewarded with fewer crowds and views just as breathtaking along the Scenic Drive of the Walhalla Plateau, which includes stops such as Point Imperial, the highest viewpoint

The Bright Angel Point Trail, which originates from the Grand Canyon Lodge, provides many sweeping views of the tremendous spectacle of erosion

in the park, as well as Vista Encantada, Roosevelt Point, and Cape Royal, the drive's end.

The original story and photo gallery can be found at the following link:

 https://www.stgeorgeutah.com/news/ archive/2019/08/11/raw-north-rim-day-dendroglyphs-deer-herds-and-the-golden-age-of-tourist-development/

FOR FURTHER INFORMATION
Grand Canyon National Park North Rim website:

 https://www.nps.gov/grca/planyourvisit/ north-rim.htm

*Winsor Castle, a former fort and cattle operation
headquarters, was an oasis in the desert for early settlers*

24

PIPE SPRING NATIONAL MONUMENT
An Epicenter of Conflict and Reconciliation
on the Arizona Strip

Many people who drive from Hurricane to Kanab on UT 59/AZ
389 can't help but notice the sign marking the turnoff for Pipe
Spring and wonder what it is and why anyone would want to live
in such a barren land and take their chances trying to eke out a
living there.

As its name suggests, one of the reasons for its importance is
because it has been a vital water source. At one time, it was also a
cattle grazing mecca.

It's always been a wonderful way-stop on the way to somewhere else, from late-19th century couples making the arduous
journey from Northern Arizona settlements to solemnize their
marriages for time and all eternity in the St. George Temple to

outdoor enthusiasts traveling from Zion to Grand Canyon national parks in the early 20th century.

In fact, Pipe Spring's location is one of the biggest reasons it became part of the national park system. The first director of the National Park Service, Stephen Mather, took a fancy to it in 1920 while traveling between the two aforementioned national parks and thought it would be a great link between the two. At the time, the road next to it was the only way between the two parks before the construction of the Zion-Mount Carmel Highway and its legendary 1.1-mile tunnel in 1930.

Mather, who had made a fortune in Borax mining, soon bought the old fort and the forty acres surrounding it that once belonged to The Church of Jesus Christ of Latter-day Saints for $5,000. Without Mather taking notice of the dilapidated old fort in the far Northern Arizona desert, it could have faded into obscurity.

But little did Mather know his purchase would start a protracted water rights battle among the National Park Service, the family from which he purchased it, and the descendants of the people who had made the area their home for centuries: the Kaibab Paiutes.

The Plight of the Kaibab Paiutes

The Kaibab Paiutes have inhabited what is now known as the Arizona Strip since approximately 1150 A.D. and controlled the area until the mid-1860s. They hunted deer and small game, including quail, squirrels, ducks, gophers, and rabbits, which provided a year-round source of meat. They also gathered seeds, berries, roots, and flowers for sustenance. Pinon nuts also added a nutritious staple to their diets.

They weren't a truly nomadic people, however. They also irrigated fertile land to grow melons, squash, pumpkins, beans, amaranth, and, of course, corn. Agriculture needed steady water supply, so the tribe set up such operations next to streams or springs, which were in short supply east of the Virgin River.

Famed explorer John Wesley Powell, who utilized Paiute guides to explore the surrounding area, remarked at how well the Indians knew their terrain.

"There is not a trail but what they know; every gulch and every rock seems familiar," he once said. "I have prided myself on being able to grasp and retain in my mind the topography of a country, but these Indians put me to shame."

Historians Robert Keller and Michael Turek devoted a whole chapter on Pipe Spring and the Kaibab Paiutes in their 1998 book *American Indians and National Parks*. It is one of the short histories of the monument and the tribe closely intertwined with it that reached a wide, general audience.

In that book, Keller and Turek detail how colonization by settlers of The Church of Jesus Christ of Latter-day Saints severely disrupted the tribe's way of life, bringing three catastrophic consequences: destruction of vegetation, disease, and loss of water sources. Settlers' cattle and sheep foraged necessary grasses and plants. Sickness such as cholera, malaria, measles, mumps, and whooping cough decimated the Paiute population. Lastly, white settlers soon occupied all scarce water sources, including Mu-tum-wa-va (Dripping Rock), which was also known as Yellow Rock Spring—or by its Mormon name, Pipe Spring—Keller and Turek wrote.

Early Pioneer Involvement

One might imagine Pipe Spring as a literal pipe spewing cool water out of the ground, but it received its name from a different kind of pipe.

Pioneer Indian missionary Jacob Hamblin and a few companions ran onto Pipe Spring during some of their travels in 1858. The story goes that during a stopover at the spring, Jacob Hamblin's brother William Hamblin (nicknamed "Gunlock Bill") was the victim of a prank, a bet that he could shoot a hole through a silk bandana tied to a tree branch from fifty yards away. Jacob Hamblin and companion Dudley Levitt laughed at Gunlock Bill's attempt to accomplish the feat, knowing that lead balls shot from a gun could not penetrate the handkerchief.

Frustrated, William Hamblin instead used Levitt's smoking pipe as a target. One version of the story states that Gunlock shot the bowl out of the pipe, but another version said he simply shot the pipe off a rock near the spring. No matter what story is to be believed, either way, the name has been Pipe Spring ever since.

Latter-day Saint convert and former Texas cattleman James Whitmore came to Pipe Spring in 1863 in his search for rangeland. He built a rude shelter near the spring and obtained title to one hundred sixty acres that he eventually planned on turning into a townsite. He built fences and corrals, planted grapevines as well as apple and peach trees.

Just after Christmas 1865, Whitmore heard rumors of raids by the Navajo, a contingent of which had escaped capture and forced removal by the U.S. Army. Navajos regularly raided the Paiutes during this time period, killing some and even taking others with them to sell as slaves. Because of this, by the 1860s, their population severely declined. A report by Powell in 1874 stated that at the time, there were only 207 of them left.

Hearing about the raids prompted Whitmore to travel from St. George to go check on his livestock with his son and a brother-in-law, Robert McIntyre.

On Jan. 9, 1866, as Whitmore and his brother-in-law tracked stolen sheep on freshly-fallen snow while Whitmore's son remained in the dugout, the two men encountered Navajo raiders at Bull Wash, four miles southeast of Pipe Spring, and were killed.

Whitmore's son reported their disappearance, which led to a posse of settlers killing a couple of Paiutes wearing Whitmore and his brother-in-law's clothes, which they had obtained through a trade. With emotions running high, the posse ended up killing up to six more innocent Paiutes that day. This event sparked the Paiutes to seek revenge in killing three settlers who were returning to Long Valley from Grafton that April.

With the eruption of Indian hostilities, LDS church president Brigham Young ordered settlers to temporarily vacate settlements in the vicinity while the Indian's ire died down. In 1870, Young moved to regain the church's foothold along the Arizona Strip and established a fort built around Pipe Spring to guard against Indian raids, which thankfully ended in 1869 after the establishment of a Navajo Reservation, so the fort was never put to the test.

Winsor Castle, as the fort came to be called (a play on words in reference to the real Windsor Castle in the United Kingdom) was named after its first caretaker, Anson Winsor, and became the headquarters of the church's cattle operation in the area, as well as Arizona's first telegraph station after first being presumed the fort was located in Utah.

Finished in 1872, the fort consisted of two-story red sandstone buildings facing each other across a courtyard closed at each end with heavy gates. The fort included slit-like gun ports, built into the thick walls in upstairs rooms as fortification against impending danger, which, thankfully, never materialized. A few stone cabins were built surrounding the fort as extra quarters.

The fort's north building was erected directly over the spring, and the water flowed to the south building. More than just supplying water, the cool waters from the spring acted as refrigeration for the dairy products produced at the ranch, including cheese. Every two weeks, Winsor took butter, cheese, and cattle to St. George. Cows were milked twice a day during the fort's heyday. Crops on the farm included wheat, rye, alfalfa, and flax.

In the late 19th century, Pipe Spring was a church farm and dairy operation, as well as the ranch that supervised the church's tithing cattle in the region, first called the Canaan Cooperative Stock Company and then the New Canaan Stock Company.

It also became a haven of sorts for those hiding from polygamy raids because it was off the beaten path of federal marshals.

Later, however, it was sold to private interests as a cattle ranch and became an important cattle buying and shipping point, the terminus of cattle drives to nearby railheads.

The Heatons and the Reservation

When the United Order of Orderville failed and liquidated its property in the mid-1880s, one of its former members, Jonathan Heaton, ended up with the property that became today's Moccasin, Arizona, just four miles north of Pipe Spring, a town which the Heaton family founded.

The Heatons grazed cattle on their land and used more land than they actually owned for the same purpose. Hurricane resident

*There are several other stone cabins once used as dwellings
near Winsor Castle at Pipe Spring National Monument*

Matt Heaton said his great-great-grandfather Jonathan Heaton
and his family got along well with the Kaibab Paiutes. In fact, the
tribe brought its sick members to Moccasin to be treated by a
"community doctor," Matt Heaton explained.

Although some Paiutes were never happy with the white
settlers on their land, they somehow got along.

Even though the two parties had a good relationship, the Paiutes
were suffering. As one of their champions, Indian missionary
Jacob Hamblin was concerned.

Hamblin wrote a letter to Powell on November 1, 1880,
explaining the Kaibab Paiute's plight, that the settlers had taken
away their subsistence by overgrazing and utilizing all the fertile
land for their own farming. Hamblin said their only sustenance
was hunting for game.

"I should esteem it a great favor if you could secure some
surplus merchandise for the immediate relief of their utter
destruction," Hamblin wrote.

Powell wrote back that no help was possible at the time and
that if the Kaibab Paiutes wanted to survive, they needed to move
to reservations in Nevada or central Utah and learn subsistence

farming. To the tribe, both places were too far from their home-land, so they remained. As Indians without their own land, the Kaibab Paiutes had no hunting rights, nor did they own their own cattle.

In 1907, the federal government finally created a reservation for the Kaibab Paiutes, eighteen miles long and twelve miles wide, withdrawn from the public domain. Its border began south of Kanab, Utah, and west of Fredonia, Arizona, and its creation irked local ranchers, who stood to lose land on which they once grazed cattle that fell within the reservation.

The Kaibab Paiute Reservation didn't follow the usual script of Native American displacement caused by white settlement. Instead, established settlers had to make room for the native population, Mary Knack wrote in her article "Interethnic Competition at Kaibab during the Early 20th Century," which appeared in the Spring 1993 issue of journal *Ethnohistory*.

On the reservation, the Bureau of Indian Affairs (BIA), in essence, created "a reservation economy that duplicated, on a small scale, Euro-American mixed agriculture," Knack wrote. "In short, the BIA directed that Paiutes must use reservation resources in the same ways as their non-Indian neighbors. A predictable conflict of interests resulted."

On the reservation, the tribe had its own cattle herd, which grew to four hundred animals by 1914. By that time, they also had forty-five acres of irrigated crops. Local townspeople protested the reservation taking their farmland, and early petitions for an alteration of the reservation boundaries were rejected with one exception. When the 1912 public survey found that Fredonia was within the reservation boundaries, that part, of course, was relinquished.

The Heatons stood to lose the most from the reservation, with nearly three thousand reservation acres enclosed by their fences. The family even petitioned the Secretary of the Interior to eliminate that acreage from the reservation, arguing that the Indians weren't really using the land. That petition was denied, but eventually, a compromise was brokered with the Heatons receiving title to 476 acres within the reservation boundaries.

The Heaton Family still owns a lot of land in and around Moccasin. Matt Heaton said his great-great-grandfather set a foundation of hard work that has kept the family close. With two wives and twenty-six children (fifteen sons and eleven daughters), the original Heatons near Pipe Spring have quite a posterity.

Before living in Orderville, Jonathan Heaton was called to the Muddy Mission in Nevada, notorious for its difficulty. Matt Heaton said his great-great-grandfather's family learned that everyone has to pitch in to make things work well and that legacy lives on today.

Water Issues

When Mather purchased Pipe Spring in the early 20th century, he convinced President Warren G. Harding and his administration to set it aside as a national monument, which happened on May 31, 1923. However, the final sentence of the proclamation establishing the monument proved problematic and began a long battle over water.

It said that in the Park Service's administration of the monument, "the Indians of the Kaibab Reservation shall have the privilege of utilizing waters from Pipe Spring for irrigation, stock watering, and other purposes, under regulations to be prescribed by the Secretary of the Interior." Even the church had ordered years earlier that one-third of the flow of the spring be for Paiute use.

The Heatons insisted that cattlemen in the area have access to the spring, and Mather promised to retain it as a public water reserve as it had been declared in 1916. Interestingly, Knack reports in her article that local settlers never disputed the Kaibab Paiute right to a fixed share of nearby Moccasin Spring.

The Bureau of Indian Affairs also entered the battle, saying that public access to tribal water should not be allowed, which began a back-and-forth between the National Park Service and BIA that would last nearly fifty years.

As the proclamation creating the monument stated, its purpose was to preserve pioneer life, and Mather wanted it to look like it did during its heyday, with orchards and gardens, but that would require a lot of water.

Ironically, Leonard Heaton, part of the prominent ranching family in the area, was hired as the monument's first caretaker, and over the water issue, some questioned his loyalty. There were even some dissenters in the NPS who supported the Indian water claim. One of them, Thomas Parker, an assistant superintendent at Zion at the time, argued that Leonard Heaton had turned Pipe Spring into his own personal barnyard, had made the monument a disgrace to the NPS and that the problem would only be solved by firing Heaton. The BIA argued that Indian subsistence was of much greater importance than the monument's landscaping.

Keller and Turek wrote, however, that Leonard Heaton, while forced to supply the Kaibab Paiutes water, never had problems with them.

"He collected their artifacts, took school children on Easter outings, and entertained them at the monument," the duo wrote, noting that he also helped them fight a fire that engulfed the BIA school in 1948.

In the 1950s, the NPS made an inventory of Pipe Spring water and concluded that the Paiute did not need or use their third share, and in the mid-1960s, the agency opposed efforts by the Heaton Family to claim a share of Pipe Spring water as well.

A concrete water agreement between the tribe and the NPS didn't come until 1972 and was achieved only after the Park Service dug a well on Kaibab Paiute land, Keller and Turek explained.

Pipe Spring Today

At the end of their chapter about Pipe Spring, Keller and Turek tell a version of a one-sided, sugar-coated story that painted a distorted picture of the monument's history and called for the monument to expand its interpretation.

When the monument was established by President Harding in 1923, it was slated to be "a memorial of western pioneer life." Based on that proclamation, the original story that was conveyed to visitors at the monument was "very Manifest Destiny-centric, focusing on the settlers and the role of the LDS Church," said Pipe Spring Superintendent Fred Armstrong.

That Manifest Destiny theme is felt by a reading of a monument brochure from 1943.

"The Mormons who settled at Pipe Spring and other similar areas can be given much of the credit for the exploration, colonization, and development of this part of the Southwest," the 1940s pamphlet read. "Under the leadership of Brigham Young, they were able to establish their culture in this land where many others failed."

Some feel that the criticism of the monument's interpretation in the Keller and Turek book helped lead to changes in how the monument presents its history to visitors today.

Armstrong said he is "not so certain" their book was what caused a change in interpreting the site. He said:

"I would like to think it has been as gradual maturing over time where the National Park Service as a whole has been striving to tell the complete story of the places we administer for our citizens. The heritage and story of the Kaibab Paiute and their relationship to the land and local springs is just as compelling and important as the story of the early cattlemen and the relationship to these lands by the Mormon settlers."

There are multiple, complex interactions and stories throughout the monument's history, Armstrong said, some good and some bad. That history, however, has come together beautifully with the backgrounds of the actual interpreters at the monument.

"Today, I am pleased to say that we have members on our staff from the background and heritage of the Kaibab Paiute, the cattlemen, and the FLDS settler families," Armstrong said.

One of the events that really helped meld the stories of the Paiutes and the early settlers was the remodeling of the visitor center in 2001 so that the Kaibab Paiute tribal culture could be a part of the visitor center exhibits. Today, the pioneer and Paiute history is interpreted, in essence, side by side.

"Contemporary life on the Kaibab Indian Reservation blends

traditional cultural values with economic development," a panel at the visitor center reads.

Thankfully, today's Kaibab Paiutes, governed by a six-member tribal council and tribal chairperson, do have economic resources. Tribal enterprises include a gasoline station and convenience store, cattle ranching operations, sport hunting licensing, and guiding, among others. They work with other Southern Paiute bands to preserve their history and culture.

Visiting Pipe Spring

Pipe Spring National Monument is located just over an hour southeast of St. George along UT 59/AZ 389.

Visitors can enjoy the displays at the museum, tour the old fort, Winsor Castle, and inspect other pioneer relics on the grounds. During the summer months, it features ranger talks and living history demonstrations and also hosts an annual Christmas event.

The original story and photo gallery can be found at the following link:

https://www.stgeorgeutah.com/news/
archive/2018/11/18/pipe-spring-day-an-
epicenter-of-conflict-and-reconciliation-on-
the-arizona-strip/

FOR FURTHER INFORMATION
Pipe Spring National Monument website:

https://www.nps.gov/pisp/index.htm

Kingman's Route 66 Museum is a great starting place for anyone wishing to explore Route 66 in Northwestern Arizona

25

ROUTE 66 IN NORTHERN ARIZONA
The History and Nostalgia of Arizona's Stretch of the "Mother Road"

"You know Route 66? It's still here!"

That was the exclamation of an excited Lightning McQueen as he speaks to his agent over the phone after being discovered by the media while holed up in Radiator Springs in Disney/Pixar's 2006 animated hit, *Cars*.

The popular movie was largely inspired by its director's own trip over "The Mother Road," and some places and characters in the movie are near direct cartoon incarnations of real things along the route.

McQueen was on to something in his announcement to his agent. Route 66 is still here and has seen quite a bit of a resurgence over the last few decades. In its glory years, the road proved an escape for drivers seeking freedom and adventure on the open road. Today, it provides the same thing for those willing to get off multi-lane interstates to traverse what's left of it.

Michael Wallis, author of the 1990 book *Route 66: The Mother Road*, described what became known as "The Main Street of America" in those kinds of terms.

"A thread looping together a giant patchwork of Americana, this fabled road represents much more than just another American highway," Wallis wrote. "Route 66 means motion and excitement. It's the mythology of the open road. Migrants traveled its length; so did desperadoes and vacationers. Few highways provoke such an overwhelming response. When people think of Route 66, they picture a road to adventure."

Northwestern Arizona is home to the longest uninterrupted portion of the historic highway that once stretched from Chicago to Los Angeles, the 159-mile span from Seligman to Kingman. A great starting point for those wishing to explore this stretch is the Arizona Route 66 Museum and Visitor Center in Kingman, where travelers can add context to their journey into a storied past.

The Trailblazers

Native Americans were, of course, the first humans to frequent the area along well-worn footpaths that served as trade routes to the Pacific Ocean for tribes exchanging treasures from all around the West, sometimes using gems, shells, stones and woven baskets as currency. The tribes that have inhabited the area for centuries are the Havasupai, Hualapai, and Mojave.

Juan de Onate was the first European of record to visit the area in 1604, and Franciscan missionaries Dominguez and Escalante came through in 1776.

Starting in the early 19th century, free-roamers such as fur trappers and gold-panners wandered in what became Northern Arizona looking for valuable goods, and by midcentury, more and more Americans began migrating to the West for what they considered literal greener pastures—the chance to own land.

In 1851, Captain Lorenzo Sitgreaves arrived and created the first technical map of the area. After months of research, he recommended that a road be built along the 35th parallel rather than along other existing trails. For his efforts, Sitgreaves earned some name recognition along the future route of the "Mother Road"—a 3,652-foot high mountain pass just outside Oatman was named to honor him.

By 1857, the U.S. government wanted to stake out a "winter-proof" route to the West and contracted with Navy Lieutenant Edward F. Beale to survey and develop such a route. True to Sitgreaves' estimation, Beale foresaw the route following the 35th parallel as closely as possible, which was determined far enough south to provide an all-weather road.

Beale and a crew of forty-four men, twelve wagons, and one hundred twenty animals set out to survey the route. In addition to assorted horses and mules, Beale's caravan also included twenty-five camels fresh from Egypt because part of Beale's assignment included testing camels in the Southwest for consideration for future military use. It turned out to be the U.S. army's first and last camel brigade. Although the camels performed exceptionally on the journey, they were not adopted for military use for two main reasons: a request for more camels was ignored because of the rising tensions that escalated into the Civil War, and many just couldn't take the camels seriously.

The result of the journey was the Beale Wagon Road, the first federally-funded wagon road in America, built at a cost of $50,000 for an approximately four-hundred-mile road. Sections of the Beale Wagon Road are still visible today and accessible from several points along Route 66.

Pioneers who started out as a trickle and eventually became a steady stream journeying along the route met several difficulties, including finding suitable water and traversing rough trails in rickety wagons. They also encountered sickness, food shortages, and conflicts with Native Americans. Due to those conflicts, in 1859, the army established Fort Mojave on the Colorado River to protect emigrants from aggression from the Mojave tribe.

The original charter for a railroad across the 35th parallel came in 1866 but was not completed until much later. Lewis Kingman (namesake of the Arizona city) of the Atchison, Topeka, and Santa

Fe Railroad surveyed the route from Albuquerque to the Colorado River, where it connected with the Southern Pacific line at Needles, California in the 1880s.

The railroad provided more freedom and ease for later migrants, getting them to their destinations much quicker and practically without hardship.

"It is no coincidence, then, that U.S. Route 66 represents much of the same freedom as did the railroad at the turn of the century," a plaque at the Kingman Route 66 museum reads. "Both share common, unspoiled terrain as well as a knack for holding the attention of the curious traveler."

The railroad parallels portions of Route 66 to this day, and its placement gave motoring Americans their first taste of "riding shotgun" with trains.

The Okies

Formally established in 1926, Route 66 was "a 2,448-mile journey to the heart of America," the Historic Route 66 Association of Arizona pamphlet reads. "Contrasted with the other highways of its day, Route 66 did not follow a traditionally linear course. Its diagonal path linked hundreds of communities across eight states and became the principal east-west artery."

At first, much of Route 66 was dirt. It was not paved in its entirety until 1938.

It was on this dirt road that one significant group of people traveled from the Midwest seeking a better life. The combination of economic depression, ill-advised farming practices, and severe drought led to the "Dust Bowl" in the 1930s when extreme storms literally carried the topsoil of farmland hundreds of miles away.

"Dust clouds several miles high blew across the plains, covering everything with fine, dry silt," a museum interpretive plaque states. "Crops would not grow, and animals and humans were actually driven mad by the wind and the dust."

These harsh conditions inspired farmers, who became known as "Okies" because they were centered around the panhandle of Oklahoma to travel west, to find their greener pastures. Their principal route became known as the "Mother Road" because of

John Steinbeck's description of it as such in his novel, *The Grapes of Wrath*, which chronicled the travails of a fictional Dust Bowl family.

In Chapter 12 of Steinbeck's masterpiece, he wrote: "66 is the path of people in flight . . . they come into 66 from the tributary side roads, from wagon tracks and the rutted country roads. 66 is the mother road."

Interestingly, according to the museum's interpretation materials, more than two hundred thousand people fled west to California during the era, but less than sixteen thousand actually stayed there.

"Prosperity was supposed to be just around the corner, but some made the long trek to California in dilapidated 'tin lizzies' only to turn back after finding more poverty and despair," one museum plaque reads.

The completion of paving the route on the eve of World War II became significant to the war effort. Improved highways were key to rapid mobilization during the conflict. The military chose numerous locations in the West as training bases because of their geographic isolation and good weather. Many were located on or near Route 66, including the Kingman Army Airfield Gunnery School. It was not uncommon to see mile-long convoys of trucks along the road transporting troops and equipment.

The Vacationers

It is from the post-war years that most of the nostalgia for Route 66 stems. This was the era when the motor-going public decided to go out and explore the country in droves, spawning a dramatic increase in roadside commerce.

The development of gas stations, motels and diners mushroomed in the 1950s and 60s and with them creative landmarks to draw tourists in, from twin arrows in the middle of the stretch between Flagstaff and Winslow, Arizona, to motel rooms that resembled Indian teepees at the Wigwam Motel in Holbrook, Arizona—one of the inspirations for the Cozy Cone in *Cars*.

Driving Route 66 was literally an adventure, and Los Angeles resident Jack D. Rittenhouse wrote the adventure guide in 1946,

The Route 66 in Kingman is home to a plethora of memorabilia for those nostalgic for lore about the "Mother Road"

titled A Guide Book to Highway 66. It became a bible to travelers of the open road. In it, Rittenhouse provided some important advice, including:

> *"Be sure to have your auto jack. A short piece of wide, flat board on which to rest the jack in sandy soil is a sweat preventer . . . Carry a container of drinking water, which becomes a vital necessity as you enter the deserts . . . An auto altimeter and auto compass add to the fun of driving, although they are not essential."*

The same year Rittenhouse's guide hit shelves, Americans also heard Bobby Troup's ode to the highway song, "Get Your Kicks on Route 66," which has been covered by numerous musical groups since.

Wallis's book captures well the glory years and nostalgia along the famed highway, taking readers on a journey along the road's entire span just over five years after the last section of interstate bypassed the route for good. Wallis writes of its heyday with great affection, chronicling the fun and excitement of the journey.

"Route 66 put Americans in touch with other Americans through its necklace of neon lights, Burma Shave signs, curio shops, motor courts, garages, and diners and cafes," he wrote.

In his volume, Wallis gives high praise to the people along the route who cared for motorists on their journey, especially the waitresses, who he said, "served up burgers, plate lunches, and homemade pie . . . with coffeepots welded to their fists . . . who called everybody 'honey,' winked at the kids, and yelled at the cook."

Wallis also detailed the perhaps less-than-savory, but still memorable aspects of traveling its lengths.

"Route 66 was also a highway of flat tires and overheated radiators; motor courts and cars with no air-conditioning; tourist traps with few amenities; treacherous curves, narrow lanes, speed traps, and detour signs," Wallis wrote.

According to Tom Snyder, founder of the California Route 66 Association, Route 66 was for travelers, not tourists. To Snyder, tourists are all about rushing to the next popular place and finding the right souvenirs, but travelers are not in a hurry, want to explore, and want to find the souvenir makers, not just the souvenirs.

In 1956, however, just as Route 66 was experiencing its heyday, the administration of President Dwight D. Eisenhower enacted the Federal Highway Act of 1956, which would authorize the construction of a forty-one-thousand-mile network of interstate highways across the country and eventually signal the death knell of the "Mother Road," which it replaced with five interstates.

Throughout the late 1970s and early 1980s, formerly vibrant towns in Arizona, such as Seligman, Peach Springs, and Hackberry, were bypassed by Interstate 40, and in a way, taken off the map and out of the motoring public's consciousness.

One of the museum's plaques explained the result of this very eloquently:

"Rest stops were no longer dictated by the unique and enticing attractions along the road, but by large signs that said so. Today, food, gas, and lodging

> *facilities are nearly identical from state to state, and*
> *the blandness of driving an unremarkable stretch of*
> *highway takes its toll."*

In a flashback utilizing James Taylor's "Our Town" as its soundtrack, the movie *Cars* depicts just such a scenario, when a freeway sprang up and bypassed Radiator Springs, causing the cars driving near the town to not even notice it.

The Association

Like many towns along Route 66, Seligman in Arizona depended on the traffic along the highway to sustain its businesses. In 1978, when Interstate 40 replaced Route 66 and rerouted traffic two miles south of town and away from its downtown, businesses suffered. Some closed, and buildings were abandoned. One Seligman resident, however, refused to take the defeat.

Angel Delgadillo was born in Seligman along Route 66 in 1927 before it was even officially christened with that name in Arizona. He was just a youngster when his family hit on tough times and were about to join what he called "The Grapes of Wrath" people, Wallis wrote in his book. As his family had boarded up their house, built a trailer to haul their things, and readied their Model T to leave, Delgadillo's older brothers got jobs playing music along the route, and they decided to stay.

Delgadillo saw the convoys coming through during World War II and that after the war, the tourists started coming—and kept coming. Even after he grew up, Delgadillo decided to stay at home in Seligman, his only time away at barber college in California. When he finished his vocational training in 1950, he returned and set up his business in his father's old barbershop, and he's been there ever since, becoming one of Route 66's greatest advocates.

In February 1987, Delgadillo organized an effort to form the Historic Route 66 Association of Arizona, the first one of its kind. His building became the organization's first headquarters.

Interest in the cause and nostalgia for Route 66 grew. People started to want Route 66 merchandise, so Delgadillo and his wife, Vilma, answered the call, selling memorabilia out of his pool hall to support the Association. In the process, it became the first

Route 66 gift shop. Today it's morphed into "Angel and Vilma's Original Route 66 Gift Shop."

In November 1987, the state of Arizona designated old U.S. 66 from Seligman to Kingman as "Historic Route 66," which later included Kingman to the California border, preserving the longest uninterrupted stretch of Route 66 in the nation. The span has also been declared a National Scenic Byway and has attained All-American Road status. The Association's inception in Seligman earned the town the nickname "Birthplace of Historic Route 66," which it proudly displays on its welcome signs.

The association renewed interest in the old road, and motorists started driving it again. In 1988, the Association started its annual "Fun Run," in which cars drive the longest stretch of the famed highway on the first weekend of May. The renewed interest helped give the road new life, and the Arizona Association's success led to the formation of similar organizations in other states.

The Fun Run, basically a moving classic car show, is still going strong with an average of eight hundred participating cars every year, even though the weather the first weekend of May can be hit or miss (one year saw snow and another year saw triple-digit temperatures), Association Director Nikki Seegers said. It attracts participants from all over the country and world. For instance, one year, a couple drove all the way from Argentina in a Volkswagen Bus.

Driving the stretch from Kingman to Seligman would normally only take an hour and fifteen minutes, but during the Fun Run, it takes hours because participants stop at many places along the way. It's kind of a choose-your-own-adventure event, Seegers said.

Even in his advanced age, at the time of this writing, Delgadillo is still the association's president and still cuts hair in his shop, Seegers said.

The Cars Connections

Needing a break from his busy production schedule, in 2001, Pixar's John Lasseter decided to load his family up in a motorhome and take to the road to get away. On his trip, he found the inspiration for *Cars*, part of which was Lasseter's own realization from

*Murals in the Arizona Route 66 Museum depict the
highway as it was in its heyday*

the trip—the importance of slowing down from the frenetic pace
he'd been keeping.

The movie would help put Route 66 back into the national
consciousness. Wallis became a guide for his team as they traveled
the route for research for the movie. Much of the history in *Cars*
comes from the mind of Delgadillo himself. Some places along the
Northwestern Arizona stretch provided direct inspiration for
actual places created in the movie:

Seligman: Some say the character of the town of Radiator
Springs resembles what visitors will find in Seligman.

Peach Springs: A map of Radiator Springs' location shown in
the movie directly correlates to Peach Springs' location on the
map of the route.

Hackberry: This general store has experienced quite a resurgence over the last few decades and was the inspiration for Lizzie's
Radiator Springs Curio Shop in the movie. Lizzie's shop's sign,

which reads: "Here it is," is a direct correlation to the sign of a shop in Joseph City, Arizona, along the eastern part of Arizona's portion of Route 66.

Sitgreaves Pass: The road and landscape seen as McQueen and his girlfriend Sally go on their first date on the highway in the mountain range above Radiator Springs, correlates to the hairpin turns (and a little bit the scenery) along this stretch of highway near Oatman, Arizona.

Oatman: It might be a bit of a stretch, but some say the tractors with which McQueen and Mater have a little fun were inspired by Oatman's wild burros, descendants of the burros from the town's mining years, which roam the town freely in search of handouts from tourists.

In addition to these landmarks associated with *Cars*, there are plenty of other blasts from the past to explore as one retraces the path of the most celebrated stretch of road in U.S. history.

Visiting Kingman's Route 66 Museum

Kingman's old Powerhouse building became a visitor center in 1997, and the association started the museum on the second floor of the building in 2001, fittingly using money earned from the raffle of a 1964 Corvette Stingray donated to the organization. At first, the association operated the museum, but then the Mohave County Historical Society, which also runs the Mohave Museum and Bonelli House, took it over.

Seegers said there are three types of visitors that come to the museum: those who traveled Route 66 as youngsters and want to relive it, those who love the movie *Cars* and want to see what inspired it, and foreign visitors who enjoy the nostalgia of one of the golden eras in U.S. transportation history. Many visitors who come through the museum have already been experiencing Route 66, and the museum helps them connect to it, Seegers said.

The museum features exhibits portraying three epochs of history along the route: the pioneer era, the Dust Bowl era, and, of course, Route 66's golden age as America's Main Street with vehicles of each time period as each display's centerpiece.

While the museum does not feature anything related to the Pixar movie, it definitely provides hints as to the inspiration for parts of the film's plot.

The museum gives younger visitors the chance to complete a scavenger hunt, looking for specific items on a list within the exhibits, and if they find all the items, museum staff rewards them with a souvenir coin.

In addition to the Arizona Route 66 Museum, the Powerhouse Building is home to a visitor center and gift shop as well as an electric car museum. Admission to the museum also allows visitors to visit the Mojave Museum of History and Arts just a block away and the Bonelli House, the restored home of a Kingman pioneer.

The original story and photo gallery can be found at the following link:

https://www.stgeorgeutah.com/news/archive/2018/12/02/raw-route-66-day-the-history-and-nostalgia-of-arizonas-stretch-of-the-mother-road/

FOR FURTHER INFORMATION
Arizona Route 66 Museum website:

https://www.mohavemuseum.org/az-route-66-museum.html

Elephant Rock near the park entrance is a popular hike in Valley of Fire State Park

26

VALLEY OF FIRE STATE PARK
Paiute Hideout, Blockbuster Movie Filming and Red Rock Playground

The landscape of Valley of Fire in Nevada is only fifty-six miles northeast of Las Vegas, but it's a world away from the glitz and glamour of The Strip in many respects. In fact, it has served as the backdrop for other planets, including Mars, in blockbuster movies.

The forty-thousand-acre park makes a nice side trip for anyone visiting Sin City, offering nature's red rock masterpieces with its crooks, crags, arches, and alcoves—a vast expanse of scintillating scenery.

It is hard to believe that Valley of Fire was once underwater as part of an inland sea, and then, at one time, looked like the Sahara Desert. The park's red Aztec sandstone formations are products of complex uplifting and faulting—remnants of shifting sand dunes from the Jurassic Period (one hundred fifty million years ago) left behind after the inland sea subsided and the land arose.

Fun Historic Stops in Northern Arizona and Southern Nevada

The earliest human inhabitants of the area date back to approximately 300 B.C., the park's many petroglyphs are evidence of their presence. It is thought people of the Basketmaker culture carved these pictures in the stone starting about twenty-five hundred years ago. Next came what is known as the Early Pueblo culture followed by the Paiute tribe, who were present when Mormons started to colonize the area at the nearby farming and ranching town of St. Thomas.

Mormons weren't the first whites to see the area, though, according to the 2010 Park General Management Plan, as fur trappers such as Jedediah Smith passed through and the Spanish Trail, widely used in the 1830s and 1840s, meandered near the park. That trail, which later became known as the Mormon Road, became the main route from Salt Lake City to Los Angeles.

White immigrants traversing this trail caused contentions with the Paiutes, especially over ownership of animals and land as the white settlers' farming activities began to displace the area's native inhabitants.

A legend surrounding one of the area's most infamous Paiute Indians led to the name of one of the park's popular landmarks. This Paiute, known as Little Mouse, was a renegade to the white settlers and even an outcast among his own tribe. The story goes that one night, Little Mouse fired on an Indian camp after a night of drinking and was locked up then ferried across the Colorado River into Arizona. Allegedly, he escaped and killed two white prospectors and sought refuge from his pursuers in the Valley of Fire. Lawmen conducted several searches to try to bring him to justice with no success because of the Valley of Fire's rugged landscape.

They were perplexed as to how the Indian could remain in the Valley for so long with no water running through it. The reason was he found a natural depression in the rock landscape that could hold rainwater for months. This little pool, not surprisingly, became known as "Mouse's Tank" for its service in keeping its benefactor away from the clasp of the law. In the summer of 1897, however, law enforcement found their "Mouse" and ordered his surrender, but he would not give in to their demands and engaged them in a one-hour gunfight in which he was eventually shot and killed.

For a time, there was a mining operation in the area for minerals such as borates, gypsum, lithium, and silica, but the future park itself did not boast significant enough deposits to mine it intensively.

The Development of the New Park

In the late 19th century, Valley of Fire became a cutoff for a wagon road into Las Vegas. In 1914, a road was built through Valley of Fire as part of the Arrowhead Trail, a highway that connected Los Angeles to Salt Lake City. An American Automobile Association official named the park in the 1920s after traveling through it just before dusk, saying the way the sun shone on the sandstone enhanced the colors, giving the sensation that the rocks were literally on fire.

Some argued that the main road should go through the Valley of Fire, believing that it would eventually become a national park, making the road a no-brainer for the U.S. government. In 1925, however, the idea of the main road through the future park was abandoned when a route farther north, the future path of Interstate 15, was found more suitable and replaced it.

It was during this time period that government officials, chiefly Nevada Governor James Scrugham, who became a major champion of the park, recognized the future park's recreational potential. In 1925, the Nevada Legislature authorized the exchange of approximately eighty-five hundred acres of federal land to become a state-owned recreation area, followed by another twenty-seven thousand-acre swap in 1931.

The New Deal was kind to the park as the Civilian Conservation Corps built the park's first facilities and campgrounds in 1933. Some of these structures included stone cabins to accommodate overnight guests, ramadas for shade, and some of the park's trails. Valley of Fire was formally opened as Nevada's first state park in 1934, but it took until May 1935 when the state legislature met for it to receive that official legal distinction. In 1934, the highway through the park became a loop road so motorists could drive through without having to see the same scenery twice.

After the CCC's heyday, appropriations for the park were meager and discontinued completely during World War II, which looked like it could signal the demise of the park and the whole Nevada state parks system.

Almost a National Monument

In 1922, Nevada state Senator E.W. Griffith attended the National Park-to-Park Highway Convention in Sacramento, California, to tout Valley of Fire as a national monument in his promotion of the Arrowhead Trail as a link in the Park-to-Park Highway. His efforts bore fruit, and the convention was keen on the idea, recommending that it become part of the national park system.

A 2009 Moapa Cultural Resources Report put together by the University of Nevada, Las Vegas, Department of Environmental Studies said that in January 1934, *Las Vegas Review Journal* Editor A. E. Cahlan said Valley of Fire "has all the elements necessary for a national park."

In 1939, Scrugham, then a congressman, initiated a campaign for the federal government to take over Valley of Fire and make it part of the Boulder Dam Recreation Area.

"The state is without facilities to develop the attraction," Scrugham told the Moapa Valley Chamber of Commerce, the cultural resources report stated.

The former governor went on to say that he felt transferring the area to the park service "by legislative enactment" could be done fairly easily.

Interestingly, discussion on the issue stalled when, according to National Park Service maps, it was discovered that some of the park's most scenic areas, including Atlatl Rock and its Petrified Forest, might not have been included in the lands exchanged in 1931. Forging onward, the Park Service presented a bill to Congress to establish a national park in the Boulder Dam area that would include Valley of Fire.

In 1941, the Baker Act ironically sought to eliminate the Valley of Fire from the state parks system, concluding that it had no recreational value, was isolated and inaccessible, but the action was shelved with the outbreak of World War II.

Transferring Valley of Fire to federal control within the Boulder Dam Recreation Area was still being considered in 1948, but opposition by prominent Nevada leaders, including Governor Charles Russell, effectively ceased talk of any more land exchanges between the state and federal governments. Russell reactivated the State Park Commission in 1952 and worked to stimulate it with state Legislature appropriations to bolster the park, leading to the hiring of its first superintendent and ranger and the improvement of park facilities. In 1955, the Park Commission unanimously voted to retain Valley of Fire as part of the state parks system and cancel any pending applications for land exchanges.

Driving Valley of Fire's scenic drive,
it is clear why movie producers felt like
it would be a good stand-in for another planet

Movie Filming Location

Since the 1920s, Valley of Fire has hosted numerous Hollywood production companies filming movies of a variety of genres, from western to science fiction. While many of the films could be considered forgettable, there were several that became block-busters and are still within the public consciousness today.

One of the first more famous movies to be filmed on location among the park's picturesque red rock was the caveman epic *One Million B.C.*, which, excluding roll-over receipts from *Gone with the Wind*, was the top-grossing film of 1940.

In 1963, the park played a prominent role in racing scenes at the end of Elvis Presley's *Viva Las Vegas*, and in 1966's *The Professionals*, a western starring Burt Lancaster, it was a stand-in for Mexico. The remains of a wall of a set piece from that movie can be seen along the White Domes Trail.

In the 1990s came the park's sci-fi turn, doubling as the surface of Mars in the Arnold Schwarzenegger vehicle *Total Recall* the seventh biggest grossing movie of 1990. It also took a turn as the fictional planet Veridian III from *Star Trek Generations*—the film that brought the original *Star Trek* and *Next Generation* casts together and was 15th place for box office receipts in 1994. Due to the movie's plot, Valley of Fire can claim the distinction of being the actual location of death of legendary *Star Trek* character Captain James T. Kirk, played by William Shatner, at the park's Silica Dome, accessed via the park's scenic drive.

Visiting Valley of Fire

A great place to start a trip to Valley of Fire is at the park's Visitor Center, which provides displays about the park's ecology, history, and geology as well as rangers who can answer any questions. Two of the most popular trails are Elephant Rock and Petroglyph Canyon (Mouse's Tank is at its end), which are short and easy—ideal for all ages. An excellent picnic spot is the Seven Sisters area, with plenty of picnic tables, ramadas for shade, as well as plenty of places to climb around on the inviting red rock spires and their surroundings. Visitors will do themselves a disservice if they do not take a drive along the park's up-and-back scenic drive to view its otherworldly landscape.

The best times of year to visit are late fall, winter, and early spring as summer temperatures are scorching.

*Visitors see plenty of varying views of the red rock splendor of
Valley of Fire State Park along its scenic drive*

*The original story and photo gallery can be found at the
following link*:

https://www.stgeorgeutah.com/news/
archive/2018/12/30/raw-valley-of-fire-day-
paiute-hideout-blockbuster-movie-filming-
and-red-rock-playground/

FOR FURTHER INFORMATION
Valley of Fire State Park website:

http://parks.nv.gov/parks/valley-of-fire

ABOUT THE AUTHOR

A Southern Utah native who grew up in Bountiful, Utah, Reuben Wadsworth is a national parks, Italy and history aficionado.

He is an Aggie through and through, having graduated from Utah State University with a Bachelor's in journalism. While there, he served first as a sports writer and then as assistant sports editor for the Utah Statesman

While his day job is a middle school English teacher at Hurricane Middle School, he just couldn't leave journalism behind and started as a contributing writer at *St. George News* in 2013. He holds a Master's degree in history from UNLV where he wrote his thesis on the history of the Zion National Park shuttle system. He moonlights as an adjunct history instructor at Dixie State University.

His favorite food is Pizza Napoletana and anything that includes dark chocolate. When not teaching, grading or writing articles, he enjoys spending time with his wife and three spunky daughters by enjoying the unparalleled scenery and outdoor recreation southern Utah has to offer, playing a game, or watching the current television show on which his family is hooked.

He lives in Hurricane, Utah.

CONNECT WITH REUBEN:
Author Facebook page:
https://www.facebook.com/rangerreub
Email address:
reubenwadsworth@gmail.com
Days Series portal:
https://www.stgeorgeutah.com/news/archive/category/story-series/days-series/

ALSO BY THE AUTHOR

Don't miss the
fascinating stories of Utah's Dixie
in Reuben Wadsworth's first book,
Red Rock Recollections, Volume 1.

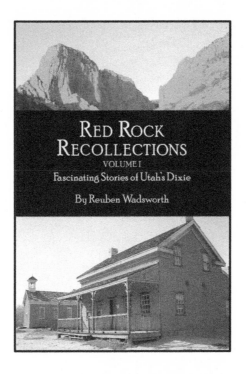

Purchase your copy now through the following link:
https://www.amazon.com/Red-Rock-Recollections-Fascinating-Stories/dp/0578559714

Made in the USA
Las Vegas, NV
07 July 2022

51238279R00152